IN PURSUIT OF A BETTER FUTURE

What You Need to Know to
Achieve Your American Dream

Charles H. Kuck, Esq.

Copyright © 2024 by Charles H. Kuck, Esq.

All rights reserved. No part of this publication may be reproduced, distributed, or transmitted in any form or by any means, including photocopying, recording, or other electronic or mechanical methods, without the prior written permission of the publisher, except in the case of brief quotations embodied in critical reviews and certain other noncommercial uses permitted by copyright law. For permission requests, write to the publisher, addressed "Attention: Permissions Coordinator," at the address below.

Jacobs & Whitehall
9600 Escarpment Blvd
Suite 745-282
Austin, TX 78749
(888) 570-7338
www.jacobsandwhitehall.com

Ordering Information:

Quantity sales. Special discounts are available on quantity purchases by corporations, associations, and others. For details, contact the publisher at the address above.

Orders by U.S. trade bookstores and wholesalers. Please contact Jacobs & Whitehall: Tel: (888) 570-7338 or visit www.jacobsandwhitehall.com.

Printed in the United States of America

Published in 2024

ISBN: 978-1-954506-82-4

Preface

At this point it is almost trite to say that U.S. immigration law is complicated and that experienced federal judges have likened our immigration system to "a "morass," Lacsina Pangilinan v. Holder, 568 F.3d 708, 709 (9th Cir. 2009) (quoting Agyeman v. I.N.S., 296 F.3d 871, 877 (9th Cir. 2002), a "Gordian knot," Aguilar v. U.S. Immig. & Customs Enf't , 510 F.3d 1, 6 (1st Cir. 2007), and "King Minos's labyrinth in ancient Crete," Lok v. I.N.S., 548 F.2d 37, 38 (2d Cir. 1977).

"Immigration Law" is not just a statute. It is many statutes, updated, modified, replaced, and clarified, not always consistently, through more than 150 years of policy changes, regulations, court decisions, treaty obligations, and cultural backlash. As one federal judge said: "divining its meaning is ordinarily not for the faint of heart." Torres v. Barr, 76 F.3d 918, 923 (9th Cir. 2020).

It is against this backdrop that I try to clarify, simplify, and compress U.S. Immigration Law, using my

35 years of experience as an advocate, attorney, counselor, and law professor, to allow you, the reader, to make considered initial judgements about the options available to you, your qualifications for immigration to the US, both temporarily and permanently, and get you into a position to ask the right questions of experienced legal counsel as you start your path to American Opportunity.

Dedication

To my beautiful bride, my eternal companion, my inspiration, my purpose, and my reason. Everything I have done and accomplished is because she believed in me. Jenni, I love you.

Disclaimer

This publication is intended to be used for educational purposes only. No legal advice is being given, and no attorney-client relationship is intended to be created by reading this material. The author assumes no liability for any errors or omissions or for how this book or its contents are used or interpreted, or for any consequences resulting directly or indirectly from the use of this book. For legal or any other advice, please consult an experienced U.S. Immigration attorney who is aware of the specific facts of your case and is knowledgeable in the law in your jurisdiction.

Kuck | Baxter LLC

365 Northridge Road, Suite 300

Atlanta, GA 30350

www.immigration.net

(404) 816-8611

Testimonials

"When I began to pursue a green card for my wife, Yi Li Shin, I called three law firms who specialized in immigration law. When I spoke to Charles Kuck I was impressed by the professionalism of his office. Yi Li and I visited soon thereafter and were even more impressed. He and Raymond immediately began to go to work. They, and indeed the entire office, were thorough, attentive, accurate and professional. Yi Li has been approved and we both are grateful for their excellent service."

— *Former U.S. Congressman, Ambassador John Linder*

****

"My husband and I both are immigrants, so we went to see many immigration lawyers and worked with some of them. No one was as good as Kuck and his team. They are very accurate and fast responding. We were extremely pleased with their work and highly recommend them."

— *Analia Gismondi*

****

"Had a wonderful experience with the professional team at Kuck Baxter Immigration. They prepared my application with unique expertise and shared valuable legal advice with patience throughout the process. Their work made me extremely confident that my case is in great legal hands, something every client would need when working through lengthy immigration procedures. For me, the team is more than immigration lawyers, as they believe in their impactful work and put all the effort into helping their clients when needed. A big thank you to Shelly, Laura, Phil, and Charles!"

— **Mohammad Keshavarzi**

****

"Charles Kuck is very professional immigration lawyer. You should have heard the way he represents his plaintiffs in court, how persuasive and impressive he is. His arguments and proofs are very precise and correspond U.S. law and ruling. I would definitely recommend this lawyer team."

— **Victoria Sevastianova**

****

"My wife was arrested by ICE because she was under exclusion orders from the immigration in Atlanta. She was picked up by ICE from my home. It is amazing what this immigration attorney can do. He got my wife's charges dismissed and got her a green card. I had visited about three attorneys who could not help. If you have an immigration or deportation problem I would advise you to go, see this guy. He is really amazing."

— *Addo Mensah*

****

"Ever since we went to our consultation visit, we knew we had met the right people. Attorney Kuck answered all our questions and explained what our process would be like. We were then assigned to paralegal Alejandro. He gave us a very pleasant experience as well. He was very responsive to my emails and answered any questions that we had along the way. I will definitely recommend this firm to any of my family members or friends."

— *Miryam Ventura*

****

TABLE OF CONTENTS

i.	**Preface**	3
ii.	**Dedication**	5
iii.	**Testimonials**	7
iv.	**About The Author**	12
1.	**Our Immigration Services — An Overview**	23
2.	**The Current Climate Surrounding Immigration**	32
3.	**The World of Investor Visas**	39
4.	**Employment-Based Visas for Professional Employees, and Skilled and Unskilled Workers (EB-3 Visa)**	56
5.	**Steps After Approval (or Denial) of Lawful Permanent Residence**	72

6.	**Family-Based Immigration**	**77**
7.	**Federal Litigation: Our Ongoing Fight For Your Rights**	**88**
8.	**Kuck Baxter — Your Immigration Partner**	**98**
v.	**Appendix**	**101**
vi.	**The Next Step**	**129**
vii.	**Index**	**130**
viii.	**Notes**	**132**

About The Author

For more than 35 years, it has been my goal to make the immigration system understandable and navigable despite its extraordinary complexity. We strive to help our clients through the difficulties imposed by a government bureaucracy that is unyielding and, in many cases, completely incompetent.

Often, the hardest part of immigration for most people lies in the *waiting*. As such, a major part of our firm's philosophy is to make sure that our clients' questions are thoroughly answered and that we make you feel that you can call on us whenever you need to. We operate with the rule that a client call or email will be returned the same day we receive it. We understand that, whether our client is a family or business, immigration is often the most important issue a person can face — we want everyone to have the peace of mind that comes from being in the best hands possible at Kuck Baxter.

An Overview of Our Immigration Services

Kuck Baxter has a team of more than 50 staff attorneys, paralegals, and other support personnel who work in every area of immigration law. These areas include:

- **Business immigration:** We assist companies and individuals seeking to obtain international employees by acquiring visas for them to immigrate to the United States and begin working.
- **Investors:** We assist investors who seek to immigrate to the United States with immigrant and non-immigrant investor visas.

- **Families:** We help reunite families from abroad or within the United States.
- **Asylum:** We help individuals obtain asylum from dangers in their home country.
- **Removal:** We assist individuals who are looking to stay in the United States when they face removal proceedings.
- **Federal Litigation:** We represent plaintiffs seeking mandamus, declaratory, and *habeas corpus* relief from delays, bad decisions, and unlawful detention. We have successfully done this in hundreds of cases in federal court.

Kuck Baxter is also part of the **Alliance of Business Immigration Lawyers (www.abil.com),** a network of immigration lawyers in virtually every country in the world, so that all of us can service our clients' worldwide immigration needs.

My Personal Experience

My initiation into immigration law came when I was a new lawyer still waiting for the bar exam results. A colleague I had at the time asked if I would like to handle an asylum case *pro bono*. I told him I did not know anything about immigration law, but he assured me this wouldn't necessarily be an issue. I continued, telling him I was not even officially a lawyer yet. Still, he insisted. "That's okay, I can supervise!" So I went on to take the case and won asylum for my client — before I even passed the bar!

I did not initially intend to get into immigration law, but after that experience, I fell deeply in love with it. In hindsight, it is not at all surprising that immigration law came so naturally to me: growing up in an immigrant household drew me to this practice area, even perhaps without me realizing it. I spent many of my younger years living with my grandparents, who were immigrants from Germany prior to World War II. Reflecting on this experience, I realize I may have taken it for granted, presuming it was a common American experience. Moreover, I had the privilege of serving as a missionary in Peru from 1981 to 1983, a period marked by significant civil unrest in a country I grew to cherish and, in many ways, regard as a second home. Upon returning to the United States, I gained a renewed appreciation for the abundance of liberty, opportunity, and safety that America offers.

I have since recognized that these experiences, although not unique to me, were transformational in bringing me from a place of taking the United States for granted to one of wanting to share its abundance with those willing to make the sacrifice of leaving their own land and families to immigrate to it. I came to understand that a way I could do this was by reaching out to immigrants from around the world and helping them access these opportunities.

Regrettably, our immigration system is in disarray. It's not just due to the continuous influx of individuals entering illegally at the border, but also because there isn't a safe, efficient, and legal pathway for those seeking entry. The very agencies tasked with serving immigrants often seem to work against them, denying entitled benefits and more. Holding these agencies accountable often requires litigation in federal court.

Thankfully, our firm has been at the forefront of this battle for over 35 years, making it an integral part of our services. We've witnessed firsthand how the government can trample over individuals given the opportunity, with the federal courts often serving as the only barrier. That's why we are dedicated to safeguarding our clients, offering the support needed to navigate every aspect of the immigration process, whether or not litigation becomes necessary.

My Commitment To My Clients

Every day, I am deeply involved in shaping the fabric of America by guiding individuals towards realizing the American Dream through immigration and naturalization. Beyond this, I actively work to influence the very laws that govern these processes. I firmly believe that being an exceptional immigration attorney goes beyond mere legal expertise; it also requires the ability to shape and influence legislation.

My commitment to this belief is evident in my past roles as National President of the American Immigration Lawyers Association (AILA) from 2008 to 2009 and as president of the Alliance of Business Immigration Lawyers (ABIL) from 2010 to 2014. Currently, I serve on the boards of both organizations.

To further this mission, I spend significant time in Washington, D.C., engaging with senators and congressmen to discuss solutions for our immigration system. Unfortunately, many are hesitant to enact meaningful changes, resulting in stagnation for almost 35 years as both parties often benefit from the status quo, using immigration as a political wedge issue.

Nevertheless, engaging with lawmakers remains crucial, and I maintain hope that we can reform our broken immigration system in the 21st century. My dedication to this cause is unwavering, and I am committed to seeing it through.

Overcoming Challenges

Having read *The E-Myth* by Michael E. Gerber, I recognized the power of systemization in streamlining complex processes into a systems based approach. Applying this principle to immigration law, I discovered that by implementing precise systems, we can simplify otherwise intricate procedures.

As technology has developed, we have developed a system that makes things as easy for our clients as possible by:

- Systemizing the process.
- Having intuitive checklists to follow.
- Using online databases to receive and send documents.
- Providing easy-to-understand sample documents.
- Suggesting methods for gathering information quickly.

When you choose to partner with us, simplicity becomes the hallmark of your immigration process. Your involvement is often as straightforward as uploading relevant documents into our secure online database. From there, we take the reins — utilizing the information you provide to generate forms, compile support documents, and assemble submission packages. Unlike the archaic nature of how the government still handles things, we seamlessly bridge the gap so you experience things in a 21st-century-friendly way.

With 35 years of navigating immigration law complexities, we understand that exceptional customer service is as crucial as legal proficiency. Our commitment to detail-oriented service distinguishes us, ensuring your journey is not just about legal matters but also about feeling fully supported throughout.

We provide clear guidance on what you need and where to find it, saving you valuable time and ensuring everything is handled correctly in the most efficient manner possible. With just a click, you can easily check the status of your case anytime. Our communication channels are always open, with no additional charges for calls. Whether it's via email or social media platforms like Facebook, LinkedIn, YouTube, Twitter, and TikTok, we are here to provide information and connect you with our lawyers and paralegals in the way that suits you best, making the entire process more accessible and stress-free.

Finally, we genuinely believe in telling our clients nothing but the truth. One of the best ways to solve your problems is to tell you that your problem is unsolvable. There are a lot of unsolvable problems in immigration law, which can lead to people chasing their tails, getting deceived, and spending money on things they do not need. Unfortunately, the reality is that sometimes there may not be a way to fix your particular immigration issue, and you should know that before spending thousands of dollars. We don't let this happen. Instead, we'll tell you upfront what we can or cannot resolve for you.

This Book Is For You

Immigration is often far too complicated when it need not be so. At least a dozen times a day, I have conversations with people who have been given misinformation or outright lies about our immigration system — and the dancing lawyers of TikTok and social media in general are not helping! The only way to combat this is to put the truth out there and explain how the system actually works. I want to put that information into the hands of the people who need it most — people just like you.

What is more, this book is not solely for individuals directly encountering the immigration system. It's also crafted to empower the everyday reader with an understanding of the truth, equipping you with information that helps you to be engaged when political issues arise. Whether you are curious about the perceived crisis at the border, the motivations behind illegal immigration, or the constraints on employer hiring practices, this book aims to shed light on these complexities.

Indeed, part of my strategy and commitment to fostering genuine and enduring change is to empower both everyday Americans and immigrants to advocate for reform. Yet, change remains elusive until there's a collective understanding of the necessary adjustments and a unified vision for a brighter future. My hope is that this book will serve as a tool to facilitate this understanding and inspire a shared vision for positive transformation.

CHAPTER 1

OUR IMMIGRATION SERVICES — AN OVERVIEW

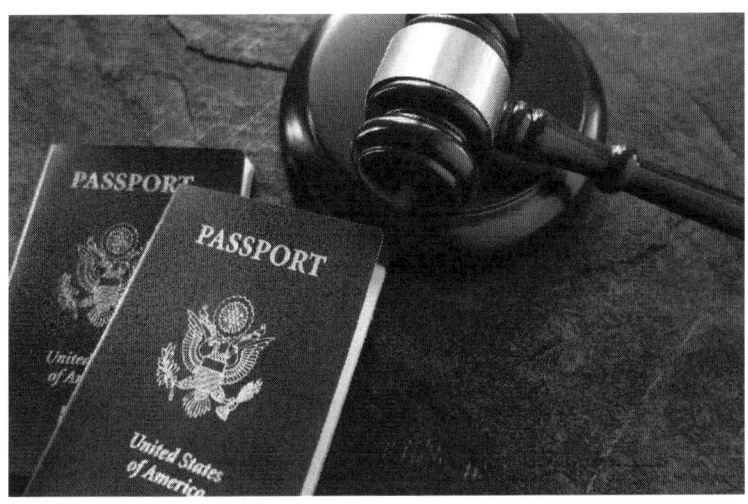

Navigating immigration law is inherently intricate, and this is only compounded by the individualized nature of each person's journey and circumstances. At our law firm, we recognize the complexity inherent in this field and the diverse paths available to achieve immigration goals.

Despite these challenges, our firm is dedicated to delivering top-notch representation that secures favorable outcomes for our clients, regardless of their unique situations. We pride ourselves on supporting our clients every step of the way, striving to make the process as seamless as possible. This commitment extends across various areas of immigration law, which we'll go into detail on here…

Employers And Employees with Business and Professional Visas

I have represented employers in large publicly traded companies, small businesses, and sole proprietorships over my career. Our firm helps these employers navigate the extraordinarily complex visa process and successfully secure the immigration status of their newly hired employees. These work visa types include:

- H-1B visas for technical workers, engineers, accountants, or even lawyers;
- L-1 visas for intra-company transferees for multinational companies; and

- E-2 investor visas for the investors or the employees of companies that are invested in the United States; and
- O-1 Visas for "extraordinary ability" employees.

We have also handled many O-1 extraordinary ability visas for people with unique experiences that an employer needs but who do not qualify for other visas.

Leveraging the visa for individuals with extraordinary ability under the O-1 visa can be a potent resource for employers. While some employers may hesitate, concerned that their employees may not meet the stringent criteria defined by American immigration law, conducting a thorough analysis of their background, achievements, and contributions is often worthwhile. At times, you might simply overlook the true value of an individual and their capabilities simply because you are too closely involved to fully appreciate their worth. Fortunately, that's exactly where we come in, ensuring that you and your prospective employee are on the smoothest path to visa approval possible.

Labor Certifications

Over the past 35 years, we've successfully handled over 10,000 labor certifications for employers and employees across the United States. These certifications are vital for individuals seeking immigration in the EB-3 and EB-2 categories — *but what exactly are they?*

To qualify for immigration, employers must demonstrate the absence of available, qualified workers in the United States for the position intended for the immigrating employee. The only exceptions are if the employee qualifies for a national interest waiver or possesses extraordinary ability as a direct applicant. Importantly, the employee must not have been physically present in the United States at the start of this process.

Fortunately, our firm has established efficient systems that streamline this process for employers. Currently, employers typically spend no more than an hour of their time over the span of the year or two it takes to complete. We maintain regular communication with immigrating employees throughout the entire process, ensuring they feel supported and informed without overwhelming them with the intricate details.

International Immigrant Investors (EB-5)

EB-5 visas are used by investors seeking permanent residence in the United States. To qualify for this visa, an investor must invest at least:

- $800,000 in a U.S. Regional Center, essentially as a limited partner; or,
- $1.2 million in a new business in America, creating at least ten American jobs.

While this program has been remarkably effective for many, there are some considerable issues with it. Initially established in 1990 with a great deal of fanfare, EB-5s have since become mired down in bureaucracy and significant challenges, so much so that you'll likely need someone with at least 30 years of experience handling them to help you navigate the excessively complicated process.

Consular Representation

Since the early 2000s, lawyers have not been allowed inside United States consulates to stand with their clients and advocate for them during visa proceedings.

Due to this, many U.S. immigration attorneys have never even been to a U.S. consulate. This is where experience truly counts and our firm distinguishes itself.

Prior to the "ban" on lawyers, I attended consular interviews. I also maintain relationships with consular officials throughout the world and routinely assist our clients in exceedingly difficult consular matters. These matters can include:

- Assisting people impacted by instances of cultural backlash, such as the "Muslim ban" under the Trump administration (as of 2024, this has yet to be tossed to the ash heap of history);
- Requiring a 212(d)(3) waiver; and,
- Preparing clients for student or visitor visa interviews.

We specialize in these matters and have a great deal of experience in them, enabling us to deliver positive results for our clients.

Naturalization

Helping people through naturalization is a cornerstone of our practice, both in terms of volume and the profound impact it has on our clients' lives and American society as a whole. While citizenship is often a straightforward process that many can handle without legal assistance, certain circumstances can complicate matters, like cases dealing with derivative citizenship or citizenship through birth. Partnering with a lawyer can streamline the process and paperwork, making the transition to your new permanent home in the United States much smoother. Luckily, we're here to provide the guidance and support needed for a successful naturalization journey.

Federal Court

A crucial aspect of our practice involves representing clients in federal court when dealing with agencies like USCIS (United States Citizenship and Immigration Services), ICE, the State Department, and Customs and Border Protection. Unfortunately, these agencies often either abuse or misapply the law, or fail to fulfill their duties as required, leaving us with no choice but to advocate for our clients in court.

Here's a good example of this: At the height of the COVID-19 pandemic, the Trump administration went as far as to attempt to shut down legal immigration. And, they were successful to an extent. In 2020, the fewest number of legal immigrants were approved to enter the United States since 1882. One of the ways Trump and his minions did this was by simply stopping the issuance of visas, not even excluding fiancé visas.

Not one to stand idly by, our firm filed litigation in federal court against the Department of State on behalf of almost 2,000 people waiting on fiancé visas. In the very first decision by a federal court, the court ruled that the State Department did not have a legal right to not issue visas, particularly in the context of K-1s or fiancé visas. As a result, thousands of people were able to proceed with getting married as they had planned during the COVID-19 pandemic.

The truth is, even when the government does not do things with malicious intent, it makes mistakes, and sometimes, the only place to correct those mistakes is in a federal court. We have filed mandamus actions, which are essentially actions to force the government to do its job. We have also filed declaratory judgment actions, which are designed to overturn erroneous legal decisions by the government. We have been extraordinarily successful in each of these areas.

We have also used our federal court experience to secure people's release from unlawful and prolonged detention under the Trump and Obama administrations. Both administrations held individuals who were not subject to detention and, particularly, not subject to mandatory detention. The administrations were not listening to reason, so we had to go to federal court and file petitions for a writ of habeas corpus to secure the release of our clients.

These are important experiences for my firm and me to have. Without them, I would not be able to deliver the same quality and breadth of service to my clients, especially if the political situation of the day turns south and you get caught in the middle of it — and if working in immigration law for over three decades has taught me anything, it is that things always go wrong.

CHAPTER 2

THE CURRENT CLIMATE SURROUNDING IMMIGRATION

In 2024, we are nearing the end of President Biden's first term. With him on the ballot again in 2024, it is possible that he will be re-elected and serve another four years. The only promise regarding immigration reform I can recall Biden making during his 2020 campaign was that he "wouldn't be Trump" (which would be a nightmare for immigrants, legal and undocumented). What a second Biden term may look like on the immigration front is obviously yet to be seen, but if it's anything like his first, I think it's relatively safe to say nothing will really change, if at all. The reality is that, despite the talk, the Biden administration has effectively done nothing to improve immigration law. They have made a tweak here and there but have not done what is needed — to usher in a monumental change to the system.

In fact, the Biden administration has arguably made the system *worse* in many ways. For example, when President Biden took office, the EB-5 investor program was in the midst of being revised by Congress. Consequently, the authority to issue green cards to EB-5 investors faced partial suspension. However, the Biden administration interpreted this as a complete cessation of work on EB-5 cases, which was not entirely accurate. As a result, I had to litigate on behalf of numerous clients who had filed EB-5 petitions and made substantial investments in the economy in 2018 and 2019, yet still awaited their green cards years later.

As noted earlier, the environment for immigrant investors is terrible. The system takes five years to adjudicate the initial investment and the source of funds before the individual can apply for an adjustment of status. So, not only do many people not have a green card who should, but their money is also tied up in an investment for up to seven to ten years in some cases!

For regular business and investor visas — E-2, H-1B, or L visas — the news isn't much better. H-1B visas are capped at 85,000 by Congress every year. Of these, 65,000 are allocated to bachelor's degree holders and 20,000 to people with U.S. master's degrees from non-profit institutions.

A glaring problem no politician seems to be aware of is that in 2024, there is a massive labor shortage in America, particularly in business, STEM, and service-related positions. What does this mean? It means that there isn't anyone available to fill the six million jobs currently open in America. An obvious solution would be to bring in qualified immigrants, yet we limit that every year to only 65,000 visas.

Moreover, we currently use a lottery system for these H-1B visas. For the 2024 fiscal year, there were almost 750,000 applications for the 85,000 available slots. For the 2025 fiscal year, it's believed this number will be significantly lower because individuals can no longer apply for this visa through multiple employers. In the past, this wasn't the case. These multiple applications significantly increased the chances of someone getting an H-1B visa. Contrast this with someone who only has one employer applying for them; they have less than a 15% chance of being selected, according to studies that have been done on this issue.

On top of this disaster, federal agencies responsible for family-based immigration, namely the USCIS and Department of State, stopped working on family-based visas during the COVID-19 pandemic. Most don't know this, but most family-based visas that are not marriage-based come through consulates — and most consulates were closed for two years— so the country virtually had no extended-family immigration for two years. This translates to no parents, siblings, or children immigrating from abroad *simply because consulates were not open to conduct the necessary interviews.* Unfortunately, this climate remains hostile even now, although conditions are improving, albeit slower than they should.

Fortunately, even though these problems paint a grim portrait of immigration in the United States, the Biden administration is making *some* progress. It naturalized a record number of people in 2023 and issued almost the total number of business visas possible. It projects that it will issue all the visas it can in the coming fiscal year as well.

Challenges Our Clients Face Today

One of the biggest challenges that international immigrant investors face today is the cost. The USCIS intends to raise filing fees from $5,000 to almost $15,000. For the applicant, this 200% price hike just to wait in line for years is understandably hard to stomach. *Why is this happening?* Believe it or not, the USCIS is funded principally by funds it collects from fees people pay to it. On top of this, like so many other employers in America, the USCIS cannot seem to fill job vacancies or create new positions to address the workload it's bogged down by.

In 2023, the USCIS created a work-from-home service center to process humanitarian cases. But so far, this has not produced tangible results. Since the USCIS is understaffed, it cannot manage the record-setting number of petitions that are being filed in a timely and efficient manner. This, in turn, opens a lot more of these cases up to being handled through the courts than was ever intended or has been the norm thus far.

Another challenge most United States employers have is that they've never navigated the U.S. immigration system before. As a result, many have an understandable sense of hesitancy when considering using the U.S. immigration process to begin with. Others aren't sure of what to expect when trying to sponsor an employee to come to the U.S.

For example, there is currently a strong demand for lesser-skilled workers, such as landscapers or restaurant workers. The H2B visa is available to people who fall into these categories but is capped at 66,000 per year. What's more, the lottery process used for these limited visas takes a lot of time to prepare. These visas are only granted twice a year, (on April 1st and October 1st), and you must prepare for these dates about ten months in advance. To put it in more concrete terms, if you were petitioning to immigrate to the United States on this basis, you would need to know no later than January who you wanted to have work for you in October. Clearly, the system is not designed in such a way that it effectively meets the practical realities of being an employer.

Our current employment-based immigration system was last updated in 1990. Although I was already a lawyer in 1990, some people reading this book had not even been born yet. To give an even more descriptive point of reference that illustrates how much the world has changed since then: in the early 1990s, I did not have a cellphone, let alone a computer. I was still dictating things to be transcribed by the one person who could use a keyboard on the one massive computer at the office. That is how old immigration law is in America, and, unfortunately, you just cannot effectively run a 21st-century business with 20th-century immigration law.

Chapter 3

The World of Investor Visas

There are three types of investor visas:

1. EB-5 Immigrant Investor Program
2. E-2 Non-Immigrant Investor Program
3. L-1 Visa for Intra-company Transferees

EB-5 Immigrant Investor Program

The EB-5 visa program often garners significant attention from abroad. Many countries offer what's known as a golden visa, allowing individuals to obtain residency by making a substantial investment, with a pathway to eventual citizenship. The United States introduced its version of the golden visa program as part of the Immigration Act of 1990, directly responding to the United Kingdom's handover of Hong Kong to the People's Republic of China. Anticipating that many affluent people in Hong Kong would seek relocation outside of China following the 1997 turnover, the U.S. initiated this program — partially because Australia and Canada had already established similar programs to attract high-net-worth individuals, prompting the United States to follow suit to remain competitive. Thus, the EB-5 program was created, emerging somewhat impulsively in response to these geopolitical shifts.

Initially, the EB-5 program was straightforward: immigrants could invest $500,000 in a new business situated in a rural or high-unemployment area, or $1,000,000 in an urban or non-high-unemployment area. Notably, a "new business" today is defined as one established after 1990. The premise was that these investors would either establish a new enterprise or invest in an existing one, thereby generating at least ten jobs for

American citizens. Crucially, these ten jobs needed to be created within two years of entering the United States on the EB-5 permanent conditional resident green card. This timing was significant, as investors were not obligated to create jobs until their immigration status transitioned to permanent residency.

During its initial decade, the EB-5 visa program didn't fully utilize its allocation of 10,000 visas annually, with only a few hundred EB-5 visas issued each year. This trend continued until around 2008, revealing the program's failure to attract its intended demographic, if anyone at all. To address this, modifications were proposed, particularly concerning the nature of investments.

Primarily, Congress introduced the Regional Center initiative as a solution. This program enables an independent company to establish a limited partnership, serving as the managing general partner. Investors can then contribute to the business. In 2022, Congress increased the minimum investment amount to $900,000. For instance, 20 individuals could each invest $500,000, totaling $10,000,000 to develop a luxury hotel.

One of the key advantages of the Regional Center initiative is its broader job creation criteria. Instead of requiring ten direct jobs per investor, both direct and indirect job creation are counted towards the requirement. Furthermore, investors are not required to actively participate in the investment, further enhancing its appeal. These factors contributed to a significant surge in the popularity of the EB-5 program.

Ironically, this happened in parallel to a significant portion of the Chinese population making a sizable amount of money and starting to look to secure prospective immigration options in case political issues significantly worsened in China. This phenomenon caused a backlog of applicants and an extensive waiting period of 15 to 20 years between investing and receiving a green card.

Naturally, there are some glaring problems with this. For one, a business may not even be *in business* 20 years after it was started. What happens then? Fortunately for many, the EB-5 is a readily available process to obtain permanent residence. However, the processing times still average around five years. As such, it is vital you understand that you are going to have to wait roughly this long after making a direct investment from outside of the United States until you receive your green card. If you are legally in the United States, you can file for permanent residence with your EB-5 filing. Nevertheless, this places you in quite the state of uncertainty, as the USCIS will not make a formal decision on your case for five years.

This requires that you ensure your business is in constant operation, making requisite investments, and following through to create the required employment opportunities. Assuming this is fulfilled, you can file a removal of conditions petition two years later. Still, current processing times for the petition to remove conditions range from three to five years — and eligibility for full-time permanent residency and eventual naturalization is contingent upon successfully removing these conditions, so you must handle this situation with the utmost caution.

In any case, it's important to keep in mind that, with an EB-5 visa, you are not likely to get American citizenship for at least a decade, in large part due to the processing delays at the USCIS. And if you have partnered with a skilled immigration attorney, ensure they do as I do in these circumstances: verify that there is not a better path for you to achieve American citizenship. There's a decent chance other options, such as multinational manager executive EB-1 visas, L1A visas, and others, may work much better for you. Maintain a sense of flexibility in your strategy here and consider all options carefully. While the EB-5 pathway offers a relatively straightforward route to obtaining a green card, the process can be significantly prolonged as compared to other options that may be available to you.

E-2 Non-Immigrant Visa Program

Unlike the EB-5, the E-2 non-immigrant visa program does not have a minimum investment amount as part of the deal. Instead, E-2 non-immigrant investment visas require three straightforward things:

1. Substantiality

You must show that your investment is sufficient to run the business it was invested in. If you are creating or buying a bank, for example, you'd need something along the lines of at least ten million dollars on hand. If you are opening an investment consulting company, on the other hand, you may only need $10,000 to buy computers and office space. There is no magic number here — it just depends on the country you're from and your long-term goals.

2. Marginality

In addition to substantiality, you must show that you have enough money to sustain yourself should you lose your investment. Put more simply, you cannot sink every penny to your name into your investment — you will not pass the marginality test. To qualify, you must be able to show that you have enough money to make the investment and keep yourself financially afloat along the way.

3. Source of Funds

This criterion requires that you show that you made your money in a legal manner. This is an especially critical issue for EB-5 and E-2 visas. You generally cannot use borrowed money to invest in an

EB-5 or E2 program unless it is personally secured by your signature. This criterion goes far to catch any attempts to violate it by borrowing funds.

Another point of difference between the E-2 and EB-5 program is the fact that the E-2 does not necessarily demand you create any jobs. While not strictly required, you are typically less likely to get your E-2 visa approved if your business does not create any jobs. To mitigate this, it's wise to add at least three employees over five years. What's more, the E-2 Visa does have a business plan requirement.

Applicants typically apply for E-2 visas at American consulates abroad, where the deliberation process typically takes 60 to 90 days. Upon approval, your E-2 visa is issued, valid for five years. During this period, you have the freedom to enter and exit the United States as needed.

Each time you enter the country on your five-year visa, you're admitted for any period of time, up to two years. While you must depart before the two-year limit, you can re-enter on the same E-2 visa and extend it for an additional two years. Consequently, you can technically stay in the United States for up to seven years on an E-2 visa.

Another benefit of the E-2 investor visa is that you can change your immigration status from visitor, student, or another visa, like an H-1B, if you're already in the United States. It's worth mentioning, however, that if you do, you'll need to resubmit your application the first time you leave the country and, in a sense, start over from the beginning — at the U.S. Consulate.

L-1 Intra-Company Transferee Visa Program

Another frequently better alternative to EB-5 and E-2 visas is the L1 visa. This visa was designed so that a company abroad could open a subsidiary or sister company in the United States and be able to transfer managers, executives, and workers with specialized knowledge to work in the U.S.

If you own a foreign business with a staff of around five to ten employees and aspire to relocate to the United States as the manager, director, and president of the company, the L-1 visa is a simple way to facilitate this. Like E-2 visas, L-1 visas do not require a minimum investment. All you need is a lease, a detailed business plan, and evidence of some source of funding. However, your foreign company must continue to function at the same time.

If issued an L-1 visa, you will be able to come and stay in the United States for one year. Approximately 30-60 days before the end of that year, you will have to apply for a three-year extension. Chances are more likely than not that the USCIS will approve it, assuming you have:

- Ten employees in the U.S., at least two of whom are management-level with at least the equivalent of a bachelor's degree;
- Actively conducted business in the U.S.; and,
- Have hired American workers.

As soon as you receive this extension, you can apply for an employment-based first preference multinational manager or executive (MME) immigrant visa or, in other terms, a green card. The same criteria apply to the MME immigrant visa as the L-1A visa extension. After applying and approval, your green card will be immediately available to you. Unlike the EB-5, you won't need to wait five to ten years; instead, you'll wait three to four years at most.

Although the L-1 visa requires operating an existing business in a foreign country with obvious costs and considerations, the advantages of the L-1 visa are clear and substantial, particularly when compared with the EB-5. If you own an active business abroad, it's wise to thoroughly explore the L-1 visa as a prompt pathway for immigration to the United States.

Leveraging an Investor Visa as a Pathway Permanent Residency in the United States

The ultimate purpose of an EB-5 visa is to get permanent residence. E-2 visas, on the other hand, do not lead to permanent residence. In fact, it's unlikely you'll get permanent residency if you are on an E-2 visa unless you reinvest your business profits into the business to meet the $1.2 million investment threshold. Because of this, we recommend that spouses of those who come to the United States on an E-2 visa get a job and have their employer go through the green card/labor certification process (EB-3 visa) so their entire family can obtain permanent residence.

One notable advantage of E-2 and L-1 visas is that the accompanying spouse of the principal applicant has the freedom to work wherever they choose. This flexibility makes this approach highly recommended. In the case of E-2 investors, this strategy is particularly beneficial, as without a significant investment of $1.2 million, obtaining a green card may be challenging. Interestingly, having the spouse work for a U.S. employer can potentially facilitate obtaining a green card for the principal applicant and their children.

Similarly, the L-1 visa can serve as a pathway to permanent residence if the U.S.-based business grows, maintains the necessary number of employees, and the operations of the foreign company are sustained. Meeting these criteria can lead to obtaining a multinational manager executive immigrant visa (EB-1C).

Key Considerations To Keep In Mind For Investment Visas

One of the favorite conversations that I have on a regular basis is with new investors. Most have heard about the EB-5 program, read a few things on the internet, or maybe were even approached by a broker to invest in a new business. When they come to my firm for guidance, my first question to them is, *"What do you want?"*

You may want to be a U.S. citizen one day. Or perhaps you're looking for a safe harbor in case your country's economic or political structure collapses. Or maybe you just want a green card. Whatever your ultimate goal, I take great satisfaction in exploring the best options to get my clients wherever they want to go.

In these situations, an EB-5 immigrant investor visa is rarely the best option — mostly because it takes so long to get. People who think an EB-5 is the way to go frequently end up with an L-1 or an E-2 instead, some even with a direct permanent residence processing through a U.S. employer. Still, we often represent clients who ultimately choose to pursue the EB-5 route, guiding them through the process of demonstrating how they acquired their funds, their location, plans for transferring funds out of their country, and their intended investment destination.

Regardless of how you choose to proceed, you must understand that immigration lawyers are not investment advisors. As a lawyer, I am bound by federal law not to provide specific investment advice or recommend particular regional centers. This type of guidance is best provided by an investment broker who can offer personalized advice based on your financial situation and goals. Once you have decided on an investment strategy and have the necessary information, we are here to assist you in navigating the immigration process. Our role is to provide legal counsel and support to ensure your immigration journey is handled effectively and in compliance with applicable laws and regulations.

To that end, there are three things that investors need to keep in the back of their mind when considering which type of investment visa to pursue…

1. Timeframe

Reaching your end goal in a timely manner is important. Carefully explore which visa option offers the quickest path to your desired outcome.

2. Return on Investment

These are *investor* visas, meaning, as an investor, you will still want a rate of return on your investment. With an E-2, you control the rate of return because you are investing in your own business and working in that business every day. With an EB-5, you forfeit a lot of this control, especially as more than 95% of EB-5 cases are for regional centers. When a regional center is in question, you act more like a charity, loaning money, but at a 0% interest rate.

3. Risk

All this will lead you to the third question: What is the chance you will be successful in getting your money back at all? While this question is the most important to many investors, some are in a position where they aren't as concerned with this as much. The visa alone, regardless of whatever financial losses you incur, may be worth it all to you. Wherever you find yourself, it is best to have a good general sense of the answer to this question before you get started.

One dirty secret of EB-5 visas: there is no guarantee that you are going to get your money back. It is illegal for a regional center to make such a promise, and there is no guarantee that you are going to get a green card. It's imperative you know this going into the EB-5 process.

The Best Possible Outcome

Ultimately, my role is to provide you with the information, facts, and options necessary for you to make the best decision for yourself. However, even armed with all the information, it's still possible to make an unwise decision. In such cases, I see it as my responsibility to raise red flags and advise you to consider alternative paths. In instances where a client persists in pursuing a course of action I believe to be unwise, I may even choose to decline representation. Throughout my career, I've observed that people tend to make sound decisions when presented with honest assessments of their options and potential outcomes.

At the end of the day, the reality is that people seeking investor visas come in all shapes and sizes. Some are desperate to get out of their home country because it is collapsing, others are planners who want to live in America when they retire, and then there are the actual investors who know they can make a lot of money in the United States. We try to discern which type of investor you are because that will greatly shape your optimal path. An EB-5 visa would be a terrible option for someone looking for a solid return on investment, whereas an E-2 might be the best option for the investor who just wants to get out of their country. Your path depends on what kind of investor you are, and there is no one-size-fits-all approach.

CHAPTER 4

EMPLOYMENT-BASED VISAS FOR PROFESSIONAL EMPLOYEES, AND SKILLED AND UNSKILLED WORKERS (EB-3 VISA)

When Congress created our current employment-based green card system in 1990, they were quite creative. They took a system that had two basic ways to immigrate through employment and turned it up a notch, creating three additional ways. After establishing employment and investment as the two primary types of immigration, they broke these out into five preference categories.

1. EB-1: First preference category
    a. EB-1(a): Person of extraordinary ability
    b. EB-1(b): Outstanding researcher or professor
    c. EB-1(c): Multinational manager executive (we talked about this in the prior chapter for L-1A visa holders)
2. EB-2: Second preference category
    a. EB-2(a): Person holding advanced degrees
    b. EB-2(b): Person of exceptional ability
    c. EB-2(c): National interest
3. EB-3: Third preference category
    a. EB-3(a): Skilled workers
    b. EB-3(b): Professional workers with degrees
    c. EB-3(c): Other, unskilled workers
4. EB-4: Fourth preference category
    a. EB-4(a): Religious workers
    b. EB-4(b): Foreign nationals
5. EB-5: Fifth preference category
    a. Immigrant Investor

Additionally, there is an option for non-immigrant work-based visas, creating a sixth "bonus" section, if you will.

What's interesting is that some of these categories do not require an American employer to show there are no other qualified workers in the U.S. for the job in question. When it comes to EB-1 and EB-2 visas, Congress effectively says, "We don't care whether there's an American available to fill the position – we simply want them because they're the best."

EB-1A, B, and C Immigrant Visas

When Congress expanded employment-based visas in the 90s, visas for "people with extraordinary ability" were new. The idea was for the best and brightest to come to America. So, Congress created the EB-1A extraordinary ability program and allocated up to 40,000 green cards each year for those it deemed to meet standards to be considered as such. Unfortunately, Congress did not explicitly define what "extraordinary" meant, however.

In response, the USCIS attempted to fill in the gap Congress left, stating Nobel Prize winners were considered extraordinary for the purposes of immigration into the United States. There is a very small number of Nobel Prize winners, however. Not surprisingly, many of them are already immigrants to America. This definition doesn't do much to help many people come to the United States.

Extraordinary Ability

You might not think that you are "extraordinary" but if you are at the top of your field and you are really good at what you do, you probably are — you just need the correct experienced attorney to open that door for you.

Your "field of endeavor" is a crucial factor in determining extraordinary ability. A good example came from a case shortly after Congress created this law. In it, a professional golfer filed for an EB-1A as a person of extraordinary ability. This professional golfer was on the PGA tour, but immigration initially denied his visa because he was not ranked in the top ten. To very few attorneys' surprise, when a better lawyer stepped in and took the case, they got the visa approved. The attorney argued that the USCIS was using the wrong measuring stick, pointing out that there are roughly a hundred million golfers in the world, and this guy was ranked 70th in the world. Looking at things this way, it's hard to maintain that he isn't extraordinary.

As you can see, this process is more than just a question of defining terms. The key is knowing what proof to submit that shows you are extraordinary and reinterpreting terms in a way that doesn't clearly cut against the intent of the law while making your case stronger. Personally, I have done over five hundred EB-1A cases across the last 34 years. Science fiction writers, dancers, actors, athletes, museum directors, business executives — you name it, I've done it. And I have the experience to help your case, too. You can find a list of the documents needed to prepare the application here.

Another subset of first preference visas is the EB-1B for researchers and tenure-track professors.

Congress created this category because it wanted to attract the best professors and researchers throughout the world to come and teach in the United States. This is the easiest green card to get. If you're a professor or researcher, all you have to do is show you are tenure-track and have three years of experience.

Finally, as noted previously, the EB-1C visa is for multinational manager executives. Congress obviously values multinational companies bringing their executives and managers to the United States. They value them so much that they will give them an immediate green card as long as they can show that they have worked for one year abroad as the company's managing executive and are working in the United States as a managing executive with a company that has been in business for at least one year. Our firm frequently does EB-1C visas for large and small companies. The company does not have to be huge or generate billions of dollars in income; it just has to be effectively operating a business in the United States. It does not mean it is easy, but it is doable with sound legal representation.

EB-2A and B Visas

Congress wants people with higher education (master's degree or higher), equivalent experience, and those with "exceptional ability" working in and contributing to the "national interest" of the United States. There are also 40,000 immigrant visas available in this category.

As was the case with "extraordinary" ability visas, Congress did not clearly define what makes a person's ability "exceptional," but the USCIS has. If you are not extraordinary, and you do not have an advanced degree, you may very well be considered as having exceptional ability under the EB-2A visa. However, most exceptional people under the EB-2 visa have a master's degree and fall under the EB-2B category.

In both of these visa categories, it's essential to have a U.S. employer who can demonstrate that the applicant isn't displacing an available U.S. worker. However, Congress has recognized that for certain individuals, a labor market test and employer sponsorship aren't necessary. Instead, their employment in the U.S. is deemed to be in the "national interest" and therefore eligible for a U.S. visa based on their ability to contribute to the country as a whole.

Yet again, Congress did not define terms, but neither did the USCIS this time. Policy memos and court decisions are what have served to define "national interest" in this context. But what does this mean? Well, when the EB-2 category was created, the AIDS pandemic was at the forefront of the national consciousness. Our firm actually did a lot of EB-2 national interest waivers for researchers toiling to find a cure for AIDS and HIV during this time. Today, however, "national interest" can take a lot of different forms. In fact, the Biden administration released a policy memo that greatly expanded the EB-2 category especially for STEM positions.

You could be researching anything from the cure for COVID-19, working to reduce homelessness in America, or studying how to reduce the effects of climate change. I have done national waivers for various areas, such as peanut researchers (people developing ways to have a better peanut), Museum

Directors, and professional "anti-hackers." We even did a national interest waiver for a lawyer from a different country who opened a pro bono clinic to provide people with legal services at no cost to them. It was determined to be in the national interest to have legal services available to those who could not otherwise afford them! As you can see, there are a lot of different areas of national interest, especially in the field of health, technology, business, law, and climate.

In this context, innovative legal strategies can secure an employment-based second preference category visa. However, unlike the EB-1 category, where green card processing typically entails little to no wait regardless of nationality, the EB-2 category may involve a wait. — particularly for individuals from India or China, who face significantly longer processing times.

EB-3A, B, and C Visas

Even though all three employment-based preference categories each have a cap of 40,000 green cards per year, the EB-3 is by far the most common. The reality is that most people just do not have the life experience to be considered "extraordinary" or even "exceptional," and most people's work is not in the national interest. Still, Congress clearly saw a need for U.S. employers to get workers when they could not find a qualified U.S. citizen or U.S. resident. It's easy to see why when there are more than 9 million open jobs in the United States at the time of writing. This is where the EB-3 visa category truly comes into play. Through the EB-3 process, employers can sponsor an individual for any job, no matter what that job may be. You can sponsor a nanny, a caretaker, a gardener, a cook, a store manager, or a nuclear researcher. Each of these types of employees may fall under one of the three subcategories of the EB-3 category:

- Professionals (bachelor's level education required).
- Skilled (two years of work experience required).
- Unskilled (other) workers.

An EB-3A Professional Visa is for individuals who have at least a bachelor's degree in a specific area and the position in question requires that specific degree. An EB-3B skilled worker is defined as a worker who has two or more years of experience as a base requirement, while "other" EB-3C workers are those who work jobs that do not require at least two years of experience.

The greatest need our society has is for people who can fill jobs that do not require more than two years of experience, whether they are caretakers for the elderly, nannies, landscapers, gardeners, or day laborers. These jobs do not require experience, yet Congress has limited them (the EB-3C category) to a maximum of 10,000 per year. As a result, there is a relatively long waiting line for these unskilled workers. Meanwhile, as long as you are not from India or China, there is a relatively short wait for skilled workers and professionals in the United States.

Understanding Labor Certification

To get an EB-3 green card as a professional, skilled, or unskilled worker, the U.S. employer must go through the labor certification process run by the Department of Labor. In this process, the employer must show, through a series of printed advertisements in the newspaper, along with other various forms of searching for employees, including websites, radio ads, and internet postings, that nobody who was qualified applied for the position. This process, as of 2023, takes about two years, and employers are required to pay costs associated with it, including attorney's fees. You can find more details on this process on our website here.

The EB-3 visa category does not require the future employee to be in the United States to apply. For example, in a recent case we handled, a local Peruvian restaurant needed a new cook. They found a trained cook in Peru (obviously). They hired us to show there were no "ready, willing, and able" U.S. applicants for the position. They ran an advertisement in the newspaper for a Peruvian cook and showed that no Peruvians applied for the job. So, the cook in Peru entered the United States as a permanent resident (with their spouse and children under 21). Most labor certifications are done for employees already working for the employer (usually for individuals with an H-1B work visa) in the United States, but lately, there has been a growing number of applications being filed for individuals not already in the United States.

EB-4 Immigrant Visas

The fourth preference category is a bit of a catch-all, as if Congress did not want to count any higher! This category includes religious workers, ministers, pastors, nuns, and evangelists, as well as special immigrant juveniles, battered spouses, employees of the U.S. government abroad, and certain officers or employees of international organizations. There is a limit of 10,000 EB-4 visas per year. Please visit our website for more information on the EB-4 visa.

EB-5 Visas

Since we have spent considerable time discussing EB-5 visas earlier in this book, we will be brief here, simply recapping some major points. These visas are used for investors seeking permanent residence in the United States. For an investor to qualify for this visa, they must invest at least $900,000 to $1.2 million in a U.S. business and create at least 10 American jobs. Unfortunately, these visas have become overly complicated, and, in many circumstances, will very well cause you to look for alternative ways to immigrate to the United States.

H-1B Nonimmigrant Visas

The H-1B visa, which is not considered an employment-based immigrant visa, is a visa for non-immigrant professionals. This visa is not considered an immigrant visa because it does not lead to a green card. It was generally designed for individuals coming to work for a U.S. business in a position that requires a specific type of bachelor's degree, such as in software engineering, accounting, law, medicine, or another field for which you would need a four-year bachelor's degree for.

Only 65,000 H-1B visas are issued each year for bachelor's degree holders. An additional 20,000 are allocated for U.S. master's graduates. The H-1B program is run through a lottery conducted the first two weeks of March each year. People are selected on the first of April. Applications start being processed on April 1st for a start date of October 1st. Once someone secures an H-1B visa, they become "portable," meaning they can work for any U.S. employer so long as they are willing to file an H-1B for them.

One of the great benefits of applying for employment-based green cards is that your family, including your spouse and any children under the age of 21, can come with you to the United States and immigrate with you at the same time. A tradeoff is that the H-1B process itself is wildly complicated. At the same time, the approval rate is close to 95%. Chances are that if you are selected in the lottery, you will be successful in getting an H-1B visa.

A substantial portion of those who seek an H-1B visa are already in the U.S. under a student (F-1) visa. For this reason, most people go from a student visa to an H-1B visa through the lottery. Typically, they are in the United States studying. After graduating, they work for a year after graduation under optional practical training (OPT). It's at this point that they have two years to get into the lottery and have the employer sponsor them for permanent residence in the United States. Incidentally, F-1 visa holders who graduate in STEM (Science, Technology, Engineering, and Mathematics) fields can extend their OPT for an additional two years.

H-1B visas are valid for six years and can be extended indefinitely, so long as the holder begins the green card employment-based process. For individuals from India under the current system, there is an infinite waiting period for a green card in the EB-2 and EB-3 visa programs. Unfortunately, filing for residence in the labor certification program, and maintaining their H-1B is their only way to remain in the U.S. beyond the six-year limit.

CHAPTER 5

STEPS AFTER APPROVAL (OR DENIAL) OF LAWFUL PERMANENT RESIDENCE

Maintaining Permanent Residence

Once you get your green card, you can breathe a sigh of relief — you are legally allowed to remain in the U.S. for the rest of your life. Technically, your green card is only valid for ten years, as you must renew it, but this is mostly just a formality since the government updates its security features. This aside, you are considered a permanent resident of the United States of America for life.

It's imperative you realize, however, that you can lose your permanent resident status. Staying out of the country for too long or committing a crime and facing deportation proceedings are the two main reasons this could happen. But if neither of these occur, you can apply for U.S. citizenship after you have gotten your employment or family-based green card and have been a resident for five years.

Employers' Responsibilities

An employer's responsibilities in the employment-based green card process are quite straightforward — they offer employment to the applicant once the visa has been approved. You must also make sure that all the Is are dotted and the Ts are crossed on the application. Your lawyer will do this for you and protect you through the process by ensuring your case complies with all relevant laws.

Employees' Responsibilities

Upon entering the United States on your green card as a sponsored employee, you will have to work for the employer that sponsors you. Legally, you are meant to work for that employer "permanently." Of course, that isn't reasonable nor practical in today's job market. Can immigration authorities meaningfully enforce this? No. Immigration will never follow up with you about this — ever. They are never going to come to you and ask you if you still work for your employer.

However, when you apply for citizenship, you will have to put down where you worked. So, if you have never worked for that employer, the USCIS will likely try to revoke your green card. They may do this even if you worked for them but for an extremely short period, like a month, for example. Generally speaking, if you work for the employer that sponsored you for less than a year, your green card is at risk. On the other hand, if you work for them for more than a year, you have nothing to worry about. Our general legal advice is to not change employers after you obtain your permanent residence for a year *at least*.

Denying Employment-Based Visas

Employment-based visas are not denied very often, but when they are, there are patterns I've noticed over the span of my career. In my experience, the three most common reasons an employment-based visa is denied are:

- The employee lied about their prior experience.
- The employee did not have the required experience.
- The employer cannot afford to pay the wage.

A good lawyer will make sure that these issues are addressed before you begin the process so as to save everyone involved their time, effort, and money. We give an employer an employee checklist that helps ensure the visa will ultimately be approved. Fortunately, in 35 years, we have not had even one denial made on any of these grounds.

The biggest mistake you can make with employment-based visas is not doing the work upfront that ensures your visa will get approved. In fact, we are frequently hired to fix problems that were caused by other lawyers. We can spend a year fixing something that should never have needed to be fixed in the first place. In one case, we had to file seven different filings with USCIS to finally put a client back in status and get their permanent residence in the United States.

We are more than willing to put in the work necessary to clean up issues like this, but there is generally far less work to be done — and fewer expenses to cover — when you come to us to begin with. When a case is denied, you must go through the appeals process — and you *never* want to be in a position where you have to appeal. Instead, just make sure that you have the right lawyer to handle your case from the start so you do not have to backtrack and fix problems later down the road.

CHAPTER 6
FAMILY-BASED IMMIGRATION

Virtually every case that we work on has family involved as a part of the process. We have seen countless firsthand instances of the immigration system putting major stress on families and relationships. In most of these cases, the spouse is not working, is at home, or takes care of the children. Beyond that, they may be thinking that they could be deported at any moment because, of course, anyone who turns on the television will hear about the problems with immigration and see politicians using immigrants as scapegoats to rile up their supporters for one reason or another.

With all of this in mind, many of the issues people encounter in the process involve peripheral issues that family members need to address. To avoid these problems, we try to work with spouses and children to make sure that everyone in the family knows where the process is going and that we have their best interests at heart. There is nothing worse than getting ready to file for a green card and finding out at the last minute that you are going to need a birth certificate that will take you a year to get. You want to know what you and everyone in your family need upfront and have the time to get everything ready in order to file.

Who Is Considered Family

Family-based immigration is the backbone of the U.S. immigration system. In 1990, when Congress created our modern immigration system, it allowed 140,000 immigrant visas for employment-based cases and 435,000 green cards for family-based immigration. Today, family-based cases make up 80% of U.S.

immigration, and these 435,000 green cards do not include visas for immediate relatives of approved visa holders such as spouses, parents, and children (under the age of 21) of U.S. citizens.

When Congress created our modern system, they distinguished immediate relatives, defining them as spouses, parents, and children under or over the age of 21. As is the case with the employment-based visa class, Congress also created a four-category preference system for family-based visas, which are set forth as follows:

1. **F1: Family-Based First Preference**
   a. Unmarried sons and daughters (21 years of age or older) of U.S. citizens.
2. **F2: Family-Based Second Preference**
   a. F2A: Spouses and unmarried children (under the age of 21) of lawful permanent residents
   b. F2B: Unmarried sons and daughters (21 years of age or older) of lawful permanent residents
3. **F3: Family-Based Third Preference**
   a. Married sons and daughters of U.S. citizens
4. **F4: Family-Based Fourth Preference**

a. Brothers and sisters of U.S. citizens over the age of 21

Wait Times

On average in any given year, over half a million people's immediate relatives immigrate to the United States, most being spouses or parents of U.S. citizens. Despite this, backlog is unfortunately the norm. Like employment-based visas, family-based visas, are limited in number each year.

For example, in the family-based first preference category, which includes unmarried adult children of American citizens, there are only 23,400 green cards issued each year. On top of that, this figure is technically limited to 7% for any given country, because no country can receive more than 7% of the total green cards available. As a result, there are long waiting lines for family-based first preference category visas, especially for Mexico. Right now, unless you are from Mexico or the Philippines, there is a nine-year wait to immigrate as the adult unmarried child of an American citizen. If you are from Mexico, you will have to wait even longer — current wait times are up to 25 *years*.

As noted above, the family-based second preference has two categories: F2A and F2B. Between both of these, 125,000 visas are available each year. There is a relatively short wait for the A subcategory because most people immigrate with their families. Further, we do not see many permanent residents who then get married to foreign nationals. There is an eight-year wait for the B subcategory unless you are from Mexico, where it is significantly longer.

For the third preference category, married children of U.S. citizens, only 23,000 visas are issued per year. If you are a U.S. citizen and you sponsor your adult married child, you would have had to have sponsored them in 2008 for them to be immigrating today. Again, of course, the wait for those emigrating from Mexico is considerably longer.

Finally, the fourth preference category for brothers and sisters of U.S. citizens has a cap of 65,000 visas per year and the waiting period is around 16 years, with the exception of immigrants from Mexico.

As long as these wait times are, they are only longer if you hesitate to get on them. As I tell my clients,

"If you don't get in line, the wait will be even longer." It's like playing the lottery: if you don't play, you can't win. So, get in line and, who knows, maybe Congress will increase legal immigration numbers at some point in the future, causing processing times to speed up.

Sponsor Requirements

Sponsoring U.S. citizens or permanent residents must meet certain criteria in order to successfully sponsor an applicant. For starters, they must have enough money to support the immigrant. If they don't, they may have someone else co-sponsor the applicant with them. Co-sponsors must also be citizens or permanent residents who make enough money to co-sponsor that immigrant. The USCIS guidelines require sponsors to make 125% of poverty-level income in the United States. Make sure you understand the legal consequences before sighing to be someone's financial sponsor. Independent legal counsel here is a must.

K-1 Fiancé

We do a lot of K-1 visas. Commonly called *fiancé visas*, these are non-immigrant visas intended to enable citizens to bring non-resident alien fiancés to the United States. Most people have watched the television show called *90 Day Fiancé*, so they have an idea of how the system works. But, in 2024, it is taking over a year to bring your fiancé to the United States!

A year is a long time to be separated from your fiancé, so what frequently happens is that the American citizen will go abroad and get married there instead of being separated from their to-be spouse for a year. They then begin the process of sponsoring their spouse as an immediate relative to the United States. The time required to bring a spouse of a U.S. citizen to the United States is about 12-16 months, but the spouse enters the U.S. as a lawful permanent resident. Of course, because of the Supreme Court's case, same-sex relationships are treated the same way in this process.

Restrictions on Family-Based Immigration

Family is somewhat narrowly defined by Congress in a technical sense, and because of that, you are limited to the categories we've discussed earlier. There are certain relationships that do not qualify to immigrate to the United States on family-based visas. Grandparents cannot bring grandchildren and children cannot bring aunts or uncles.

If you sponsor your brother, for example, that brother's wife and children under the age of 21 will be able to immigrate. If someone is sponsored as a single adult, either by a citizen or a permanent resident, and they have a child under the age of 21, their child will also be able to come. There is one category, however, that is problematic in this type of situation.

American citizens can sponsor each of their parents as an immediate relative. If that parent has another child and that child — the sponsor's sibling — is under 21, they do not get to immigrate with the sponsored parent. Instead, the U.S. citizen's sibling must be sponsored separately by the parent once the parent gets here. This process has roughly a 15-year wait now if the child is over 21 but only about 3-4 years if they are under 21. Many times, we will see the oldest child immigrating to America and wanting to bring their parents and their younger siblings after they do so successfully. Unfortunately, under current immigration laws, those siblings will not be able to come, assuming the siblings are under the age of 21.

Any family member you have who wishes to immigrate to the United States but cannot be sponsored via a family-based visa can immigrate through an employment-based category. In some instances, it may be faster for a family member to immigrate through employment even if they can immigrate via a family-based visa. Understanding the possible path that can best help you and your family achieve your immigration goals is vital. These nuances make it clear why seeking the guidance of someone with that knowledge such as an immigration lawyer who understands how the process works is incredibly important to ensuring that your entire family can be together for as long as possible. By doing this, you can explore every option available to you, guided by a professional with years of experience handling these matters.

Risks Of Undocumented Immigration

There are a number of people in the United States who entered without a visa, are undocumented and married to American citizens. People in these situations cannot obtain permanent residence in the United States, even though they are the immediate relative of a U.S. citizen. This is because Congress passed a law in 1996 that made three substantive changes to family-based visas, essentially stating that undocumented immigrants cannot:

1. Obtain permanent residence in the United States. They must first leave and be interviewed at a U.S. consulate in their respective home country.
2. Re-enter the United States for ten years after leaving the country for any reason.
3. Ever re-enter the United States if they have been in the country for over one year, left, and reentered illegally.

These rules do not allow for exceptions in instances where American citizens are married to illegal immigrants. So, for example, a couple may be separated for ten years if the undocumented immigrant spouse leaves the United States. There are provisions in the law that enable bypassing this, however. Advanced or provisional waivers (Form I601A) allow the immigrant to be forgiven and re-enter the United States, before they leave.

As you can see, if you are an undocumented immigrant and married to an American citizen or permanent resident, it is especially important that you work with legal counsel to ensure that you comply with the law and determine what process you should follow to find the best outcome in your particular circumstance.

Chapter 7

Federal Litigation: Our Ongoing Fight For Your Rights

Historically speaking, it is infrequent and relatively rare for immigration cases to end up in federal courts. The reason for this is because immigration has historically been efficient. Only within the last 20 years the USCIS has devolved into the wildly ineffective service we know it to be today. Unfortunately, this means that extraordinary delays in processing time and other procedural issues have caused terrible harm to people who cannot get the benefits that they are entitled to in a reasonable amount of time.

When Delays Became the New Normal

What caused this to happen? Rewind to the Bush administration, when the federal government began to delay processing naturalization cases for Muslims and people from Muslim-majority countries following the September 11th attacks. As a result, cases piled up and litigation became a go-to strategy to force the USCIS to resolve cases promptly starting in the mid-2000s. The government tends to just sit on cases forever when it does not want to make an approval instead of finding a reasonable reason for denial.

It sounds astounding because it is — if the government does not want to award an immigration benefit but does not have a legal basis to deny it, they just refuse to decide the case. But this is not the only issue. Additionally, there is now the issue of the USCIS simply not having the employees, the will, or the management competency needed to get work done within a reasonable processing time.

The government publishes their average processing times per case on their website, which can be found here. This used to list a median date by which 93% of cases were officially decided. In 2022, the USCIS changed that metric, and the date that they now show is the time frame from filing by which 80% of the cases are completed. This is of no help to an individual who is not within that 80%. These dates are also wildly inaccurate and do not appear to be based on any reality whatsoever.

Because of this, people can wait for anywhere from two to ten years for an adjudication of their case. We had one client who waited *17 years* for an adjudication. When these sorts of delays occur, the individual has the right to go to federal court and tell the judge that the government should not be allowed to take a decade to decide whether they are to receive the benefits they are entitled to by law.

Recently, our firm represented an individual who applied for asylum in the U.S. because he was going to be tortured if he were to return to his home country of Afghanistan. He filed this visa application in

2013. While he waited for approval, both his father and his brother were killed. In addition, he had a reasonable fear that the rest of his family was in imminent danger. It was clear that his ability to immigrate and bring his family to safety in the United States — before it was too late — was being unnecessarily delayed, so we filed his case in federal court.

When you file a case in federal court, the government has 60 days to respond from the date they are served. We received a phone call 45 days after filing and were asked if our client could come in for an interview. Our client went in the very next day and was approved for his asylum three days later. Now, he is waiting for USCIS to approve his wife and children to join him as asylees so they live without fear of persecution.

This is somewhat of a happy ending, but the truth is, there was no legitimate reason for this case to take as long as it did. Unfortunately, hundreds of others have in essence the same story, repeated throughout my career.

I have spent the last 35 years educating fellow lawyers on how to help people immigrate to the United States. In fact, in my inaugural speech as President of the American Immigration Lawyers Association, I encouraged my colleagues: learn to litigate, hold the government accountable, and make sure that they do the right thing — even when that is hard to do.

https://www.youtube.com/watch?v=V0R1rItzLGE (part 1)

https://www.youtube.com/watch?v=-etT6wixXoY (part 2)

Of course, taking a case to court is a viable process and is sometimes absolutely necessary. However, flooding the courts with cases won't do much to solve the issue of cases taking so long — it will just move the problem to a different avenue in which it exists. There are certain cases that should *not* go to court. There is an old saying among lawyers that "bad facts make bad law." This is why you need to talk to a lawyer with extensive experience in federal court to make sure that your case is not the kind that is dead on arrival and only wastes your time.

Backlash For Filing Against the Government

Clients are frequently concerned that filing a case against the government will risk some type of backlash. However, in 35 years of litigating, I have found that the opposite is true. People who file lawsuits are treated better than people who do not. Knowing that an applicant is not afraid to sue for something that is time-consuming and expensive for the government to defend usually means that the person will be treated with respect.

I have never had the government give a judge a good reason for why it took five years to process a case. Instead, when I file a case, the government will routinely just grab the file and make a decision. Of course, this does not mean that you are going to win your case automatically, but I have never seen any backlash to filing a lawsuit against the USCIS or the Department of State. You only file for a benefit you know that you are going to get — and a good lawyer will ensure that this is the case before you get started.

Positive Change Through Federal Court Action

For the reasons above, and many more, you must know you cannot file a lawsuit against the government by yourself — you will not only want but will *need* a lawyer with *a lot* of experience. We have filed thousands of cases that helped fiancés bring their to-be spouses to the United States. We have filed to force the Department of State to issue diversity visas, the USCIS Asylum office to decide asylum cases, and the USCIS to naturalize permanent residents in cases that had been pending for ten years when it did not want to. We even sued on behalf of one of our own employees when the government took away her DACA (Deferred Action for Childhood Arrivals) status illegally. **https://casetext.com/case/coyotl-v-kelly**. We forced the government, through the judge, to give her DACA status back. Today she is a lawful permanent resident.

The truth is that it is my great joy to hold the government to account so that it does these things. This is what litigation in the world of immigration law is all about--making sure that the government does what it is required to do. Unfortunately, regardless of its motivation, you simply cannot depend on the government to do the right thing all the time.

The Department of Justice, which represents the government in immigration-related cases, has been inundated with litigation over the last decade. Due to this, they go to "their client" — the government — and tell them that they need to fix the problem because they cannot keep defending incompetence in court. So, by filing litigation, you are working to force the government to make necessary changes.

A Case Study

Due to the war in Ukraine, a large number of Ukrainians have sought refuge in the United States. Congress subsequently passed a bill, Uniting for Ukraine, which stated that Ukrainians who came under this new program were entitled to be treated as refugees, but that they would not be able to get a green card after one year, which is a benefit that refugees typically get.

When people came to the country under Uniting for Ukraine, they believed they were entitled to work – because refugees in the U.S. are entitled to work right away. In fact, refugees do not need a work permit but if they want one, they get it for free. In reality, the USCIS was charging Uniting for Ukraine beneficiaries $410 for a work permit and telling them that they could not work until they got it, and then they were taking eight months to make a decision.

So, my colleagues and I sent a letter telling the USCIS that what they were doing was illegal and that we were going to sue them if they did not fix it. They didn't, so in September of 2022, we filed a preliminary injunction which gave the government 60 days to respond. What happened? On day 59, USCIS issued a new policy that said if you came to the United States under the Uniting for Ukraine bill, you did not need to apply for a work permit. Those who wanted one could get one for free and could start working right away.

This is what litigation does: it fixes problems caused by government incompetence. By filing that single lawsuit, we were able to help 240,000 Ukrainian refugees. Stories like this are why I love doing what I do.

Immigration Attorneys Practicing in Federal Court

Very few immigration lawyers handle federal court litigation because it has no context within the immigration system. Immigration law is a practice based in policy, forms, and regulation. In contrast, litigation is all about statutes, procedures, and rules of procedure. Therefore, if you want to litigate a case, you need go to an immigration lawyer who focuses on litigating these cases.

This is why our firm is so frequently hired by our colleagues in the bar to handle their litigation cases. Since they are so complex, they require our ability to effectively communicate with a government counsel and the judge. These cases are not just about filling out a form, you must show a judge, who generally has no knowledge of immigration, how the government is wrong. This requires a tremendous amount of experience and skill that you will simply not get by filing work permits with the government.

Chapter 8

Kuck Baxter — Your Immigration Partner

Kuck Baxter is proud to say that everyone who works for our law firm is an immigrant in one way or another, whether directly or indirectly. We have a special mission to bring the best people to the United States, and we believe that those best people are immigrants who actively seek to come to America on their own! They are investors, employers, employees, business owners, moms, dads, brothers, sisters, spouses, and children. They are people who want something better for themselves, their loved ones, and their community.

At Kuck Baxter, we make that possible because we understand where you are coming from. We have been there. We work with you, we employ you, and we assist you. We make sure that you are not overwhelmed by a system that is not there to make your experience navigating immigration and America easy.

What I love about having decades of experience and a team of 50 made up of lawyers, paralegals, and support staff is the multitude of opportunities to serve in every unique area of immigration law. You cannot bring a problem to our firm that we have not already solved. You cannot bring us a question that we have not already answered.

We cannot guarantee that you are going to like the answer to your question, but we can guarantee that we will have a decent sense of how to resolve your issue. We will always tell you the truth, and help you fully understand your situation and options so that you can make the best possible decisions for yourself and your loved ones. We will help you to understand where you have come from, what your past actions mean, what the present situation is, and where you are headed. In short, working with us means you will know where we are going, how we are going to get there, and how long it is going to take.

When you hire a law firm, these are all the things you must know because, ultimately, this process is about you and your journey — and we are here to help you make that journey the best one it could possibly be.

Appendix

EB-5 Source of Funds & Document Checklist

KUCK | BAXTER
IMMIGRATION

Kuck Baxter Immigration

Source of Funds

-Worksheet and Document Checklist-

TABLE OF CONTENTS

General Rules 3
Investors Net Worth Worksheet: 4
Documentation: 5
    Identification and Biographic Documents 5
    Employment Documents 5
    Salary/Dividends from Employer/Company 5
    Investments 6
    Business Documents 7
    Real Estate 8
    Loan from a Company 10
    Other Sources of Income 11
    Court Proceedings 11
Path of Funds: 12

General Rules:

The USCIS requires that investors prove (1) that the invested capital is "lawful", and (2) that the investor has a "level of income" that has allowed the investor to accumulate sufficient wealth that would enable the investor to invest the necessary funds in the EB-5 program.

An investor's "self-serving" declarations are unlikely to satisfy USCIS requirements for proof of either lawful source of funds or sufficient funds to invest. Source of funds, i.e., how the money to be invested was earned/accumulated, must be proven through documentary evidence.

An investor should submit all (or as many as possible) of the various types of documentary evidence requested for both the investor and the investor's spouse, unless a particular category of documents is not relevant to the investor. Copies will suffice unless the USCIS asks for the original document.

It is important to note that all evidence and documents submitted must be in or translated into the English language (non-English documents do not constitute evidence).

Investors Net Worth Worksheet:

Location of assets: ☐ United States   ☐ Abroad   ☐ Both

If abroad, which country (countries)? _____

Assets

Checking Account	$_____
Savings Account	$_____
Investments (stocks, bonds, & mutual funds)	$_____
Business Income	$_____
Real Estate	$_____
Inheritance	$_____
Gift	$_____
Other (explain on separate sheet)	$_____
Total	$_____

Liabilities

Mortgage	$_____
Other Loans (explain on separate sheet)	$_____
Total	$_____

Total Net Worth $_____

SOURCE OF FUNDS FOR $500,000 INVESTMENT
*Please use additional sheet if necessary.
Of the above assets, which will contribute to the $500,000 investment?

Asset _____	$_____
Asset _____	$_____
Asset _____	$_____
Asset _____	$_____
Asset _____	$_____
Asset _____	$_____
Asset _____	$_____
Asset _____	$_____

Total Investment $500,000

Documentation Required:

In support of this application, please provide a detailed written statement by the Investor summarizing how the Investor will obtain the money for investing in the in the EB-5 project.

Please also provide as many of the following documents as possible:

A. Identification and Biographic Documents
- Copy of Passport of Investor (all pages).
- Copy of I.D. card of Investor.
- Copy of Passports of Investor's spouse and unmarried children aged under 21 (all pages).
- Copy of I.D. card of spouse and all unmarried children under 21.
- Copy of U.S. visa stamps and I-94 departure record (for Investor and family members currently in the U.S.)
- Notarized copy of birth certificate of Investor, spouse and all unmarried children under 21.
- Notarized copy of marriage certificate of Investor and spouse.
- Notarized Copy of Former Name Certificates for Investor or immediate family members (if applicable)
- Notarized Copy of Divorce Certificate for Investor or Spouse (if applicable)
- Notarized Copy of Death Certificate for Investor's immediate family members (if applicable)
- Copy of any university degree of Investor.
- Personal Résumé (curriculum vitae or work history summary) of Investor.

B. Employment Documents
- Your educational documents
- Any employment confirmation of reference letters that you have (it is not necessary to obtain letters that you do not have)
- Employment contracts (if any)
- Professional licenses (if any)

C. Salary/Dividends from Employer/Company
- Investor's Personal Tax Returns for last 5 years.
- Employment Contract of the Investor.
- Salary Receipts for the last 2 years.
- Bank Statements of the Investor showing the deposit of the Investor's salary or dividends into his/her bank account for the last 2 years.
- Employer/Company Business License.
- Employer/Company Tax Registration Certificate.
- Employer/Company Tax Returns for last 5 years.
- Employer/Company VAT (Value added Tax) Certificates and Receipts.
- Employer/Company EIT (Enterprise Income Tax) Certificates and Receipts.
- Employer/Company Audit Report for the last 5 tax years.
- Employer/Company Financial Statements for the last 5 years.

- Employer/Company Bank Statements for the last 2 years.
- Employer/Company's promotional material explaining its operations and success.

D. Investments
- Copies of all investment or securities accounts for the last three years (if significant gains on the investments or securities transactions occurred before the last three years, please include documentation of such transactions).
- Stock certificates
- Bank Statements – Please include one bank statement for each of the last three years for any bank accounts in which you maintained a substantial balance.

For all bank or brokerage account investments, please provide a listing including the following information:

Brokerage or bank name	Type of account or investment instrument	Name of the account	Number of the account	Balance in the account	Date account opened

E. Business Documents
- Business registration records for all businesses in the U.S. or outside the U.S.
- Business promotional materials, including website addresses
- Documentation proving your ownership, directorship, or officership in each company, including stock records, corporate minutes, or other official documents
- Documentation relating to sale of any business (documents should indicate the amount of proceeds you received from the sale)
- Accountant's evaluation or appraisal of business for all businesses in which you own a controlling or substantial interest

For each business, please indicate:

Name of business	Country incorporated	Nature of business	% of your ownership	Salary/income earned	Your share of profits or earnings	Amount of your investment

F. Real Estate

For all of your real estate assets, please provide the following information:

Complete Address of Property:
Listed Owners of Property:
Purchase Price: $
Date of Purchase:
Appraisal Price: $
Date of Appraisal:
Mortgage Balance Due (if any): $
Rental Income (if any): $
Date of Sale:
Amount of Sale Proceeds: $
Description of the type of real property (condominium, commercial, warehouse, etc.)

- Joint Declaration of Assets (if the property is owned by Investor and spouse)
- Real Estate Ownership Certificate
- Contract for Original Purchase of the Real Estate Property
- Real Estate Invoice/Receipt evidencing full payment for the Property
- If a loan was taken out in order to help pay for the Property, then please include a copy of that Loan Agreement along with an Invoice/Receipt/Letter from the Bank stating that the Investor has fully paid off the loan

- Deed Tax Certificate
- Contract for Sale of Real Estate Property
- Real Estate Invoice/Receipt evidencing the sale of Property
- Receipts or Remittance Advices evidencing payment of the Real Estate Property to the Investor
- Bank Account Statement of the Investor evidencing that the proceeds from the sale of the Property were deposited into the Investor's Bank Account
- Real Estate Appraisal Report
- History of where the investor acquired the money to buy the real estate. The US Immigration Service requires that the investor explain how the real estate was originally acquired, whether by loan, gift, or from savings. A written statement would be helpful.
- If the investor was able to purchase the real estate from his acquired savings and loans, then the work certificates would need to reflect that at the time the real estate was purchased, the investor had sufficient funds and money to purchase that piece of property. A written statement attesting to this would also be helpful.
- Contract for Personal Mortgage Loan from Bank.
- Indebtedness Certificate.
- Investor's Bank Account Statement showing a deposit of funds from the Bank who made the loan. The Investor's Bank Account Statement should state:
    - Investor's Name
    - Name of the Bank
    - Account Number
    - Date of Transfer

G. Loan from a Company

If the money to be invested originates from a loan from a company, please make sure to pay the money into a personally owned bank account of the investor.

It is very important to show that the Company had sufficient funds in its bank account at the time it issued the loan and remitted the funds to the Investor. This can be demonstrated through the Company's financial statements and bank statements.

- Labor Employment Contract of the Investor (if applicable)
- Salary Receipts for the last 2 years
- Bank Statements of the Investor showing the deposit of the Investor's salary into his/her bank account for the last 2 years
- Company Business License
- Company Tax Registration Certificate
- Company Capital Verification Report
- Company VAT (Value added Tax) Certificates and Receipts
- Company EIT (Enterprise Income Tax) Certificates and Receipts
- Company Audit Report for the last 5 tax years
- Company Financial Statements for the last 5 years
- Company Bank Statements for the last 2 years
- Company's promotional material explaining its operations and success
- Investor's Application for Loan from the Company
- Company's Shareholder Resolution Approving the Loan
- Company Loan Agreement to the Investor
- Bank Statement of Company showing that loan money was successfully withdrawn from Company's bank account
- Bank Statement of Investor showing that loan money was successfully deposited into his/her personally owned bank account.

H. Other Sources of Income
- Inheritance – all documents relating to inheritances you have received, including estate settlement of deceased
- Divorce – all documents relating to income received from divorce, including alimony, property settlements, etc.
- Lawsuits – all documents relating to dollars recovered in a civil lawsuit, including official judgment or decree of the court
- Gifts – all documents relating to gifts, including:
  - Gift Declaration
  - Relationship Certificate between the Donor and Investor
  - Donor's Work Income Certificate (if applicable)
  - Donor's Personal Tax Returns
  - Source of Donor's Gift (ex. Sale of Real Estate, Mortgage of Real Estate, etc.)
  - Bank Account Statement of Donor showing that funds were withdrawn from the Donor's Account
  - Bank Account Statement of Investor showing that funds were deposited into the Investor's Account

Please provide details of each gift, including:

Date of Gift:	Name of Person Giving Gift
Amount of Gift: $	
Information Regarding the Source of Income of the Person Giving the Gift	

I. Court Proceedings (if applicable)
- All documents relating to court proceedings in which you have been involved, whether civil or criminal, and whether as a plaintiff or defendant (include all official court records and legal judgments)

Path of Funds:

In addition to proof of the lawful source of the investor's funds, the USCIS insists on documentation that links the invested funds to the investor. It is critical to be able to provide every document necessary to trace the invested funds from their source overseas to the investment in the U.S. This is called tracing the "path of funds".

The following documents may be used to meet this requirement:
1. Wire transfers receipts
2. Deposit receipts
3. Bank statements showing withdrawal of the funds from one account and deposit of the funds in another account
4. Letter from the bank confirming the funds transfer

Document Checklist for E-1 & E-2 Individual Visa

E-1/E-2 List of Required Documents
Treaty Trader/Treaty Investor

Company Information

1. Evidence of ownership and nationality of U.S. and related foreign enterprise.
2. Documentation of date and place of establishment of U.S. enterprise (certificate of incorporation, LLC agreement, bylaws, prospectus, etc.).
3. Evidence of investment or capitalization of U.S. enterprise.
4. U.S. Federal EIN#, number of employees and address of U.S. office.
5. List of all affiliated offices in and outside U.S. including addresses and relationship to U.S. enterprise.
6. List of personnel in the U.S.
7. Bank statements evidencing funds to conduct business;
8. Company brochure/annual report and financial statements for both U.S. and foreign enterprise.
9. Evidence of real and operating enterprise in the U.S. (tax returns, balance sheets, etc.)
10. If new office in U.S., provide copy of lease or evidence of ownership of premises for office and Business Plan.

Individual/Applicant Information

1. Photocopy of complete passport. If in the U.S., copy of current I-94 arrival/departure record and Form I-797.
2. Detailed job description, including job title, responsibilities, supervisory authority, specialized knowledge.
3. Organizational chart reflecting the position and lines of authority.
4. Curriculum vitae/resume of applicant detailing present and past employment experience.
5. Copies of <u>university</u>-level or higher degrees (no high school/secondary information necessary).
6. Names and copies of passports for family members (spouse and children under 21) who will accompany or follow the principal applicant to the U.S.

H-1B (New) Supporting Doc Checklist for Company & Employee

SUPPORT DOCUMENTATION LIST FOR NEW H-1B PETITION (Company & Employee)

CORPORATE (Prospective U.S. Employer):
1. Full legal name and address of the company;
2. Company address where prospective employee will work (if different than above);
3. Federal Tax Identification Number;
4. Current Number of U.S. Employees for the Company;
5. Date of Incorporation for the Company;
6. Current Annual Report and/or Audited Financial Statements (*if public company obtain online);
7. Yearly net income for the Company (for the most recent tax year);
8. Yearly gross income for the Company (for the most recent tax year);
9. Full Name, Title, Phone Number, and Email Address of the company's authorized signatory for documents;
10. Corporate Letterhead – approximately 10 pages or e-letterhead file;
11. Detailed Job Description for position offered – including job title and list of all job duties (at least one paragraph); title of immediate supervisor, number and titles of persons supervised, and **annual salary** and benefits information; and
12. Lease or deed for business premises; Business Plan (* for new businesses only).

*Note: if H-1B employee will be working as **Consultant**, will need few additional documents – see next page ***

INDVIDUAL (Foreign national seeking H-1B Status):
1. Completed Immigration Questionnaire (KIP to email link to employee);
2. Copy of individual's passport biographic page, I-94, and visa page. To print electronic I-94 card, go to https://i94.cbp.dhs.gov/I94/#/home;
3. Copy of individual's current and all prior immigration approval notices (Forms I-797, I-20s, EAD cards, etc);
4. Copy of individual's resume;
5. Copy of individual's educational documentation – diploma, transcripts, educational evaluation (if educated abroad);
6. Copy of professional licenses, professional society memberships or cards, etc.; and
7. Copy of individual's last three pay statements for current employment and/or any conveniently available letters, etc. verifying prior work history.

If Individual has DEPENDENTS in the U.S. (Spouses/Children of Foreign National):
1. Copy of marriage certificate;
2. Copy of children's birth certificate; and
3. Copy of each dependent's passport biographic page, I-94, and visa page.

**** **NOTE**: English translations must be provided for any foreign language document****

Additional documentation required from <u>Company</u> for <u>Consulting H-1B positions</u>:

1. Copy of signed Employment Agreement;
2. Copy of Works Order for End User (The length of time on the work order should cover the entire requested validity period of the H-1B. If not, we must provide other contracts to cover the requested time period);
3. Copy of Subcontractor Agreements for each job location where employee will work; and
4. List of all job locations where potential employee will be working with dates of employment at each location

KBI Client Document Checklist
for New L-1A Visa

<u>Documents from Foreign Company:</u>

1. Proof of incorporation from official source (such as city or province with which the business is registered);
2. Articles of incorporation documents or equivalent (papers given by the city or province evidencing that the business exists and has the right to do business);
3. Copies of ownership documents (stock certificates or other documents that list the owners of the business or the shares of the business);
4. Company organization chart documenting the relationship between the foreign and U.S. company;
5. Current number of employees;
6. Evidence that the Foreign company has been doing business for <u>one year or longer</u>:
    a. Most recent tax returns;
    b. Copies of invoices or tax payment receipts from the past year — enough to show company is substantial and has been and is doing business;
    c. Business bank statements;
    d. Any other money transfer documents in the name of the company, again showing that the company is active and doing business;
    e. Copies of payroll records that include a payroll ledger and proof of payment of salaries to employees (must be more that two employees) for the past year — at least one record per quarter is required;
    f. Financial statements
        i. Balance sheet — this balance sheet should show enough available cash (profit from the last year) to support the U.S. operation for at least one year (there is no minimum amount, but we suggest that the amount be at least equal to the salary the executive will draw in the United States);
        ii. Profit and Loss statement;
    g. U.S. Customs documents, as applicable (if the company is in the import/export business);
    h. Ten photographs (either 3x5 or 4x6) of the interior and exterior of the Company's office/warehouse and photos of employees working there; and
    i. Copy of lease or deed for business premises, valid for at least one year (signed and dated by all parties);
7. **Evidence of beneficiary's employment for one year of the past three as an executive or manager**:
    a. Letter from high-level manager or executive in foreign business describing beneficiary's managerial position abroad, including the specific job duties/functions along with the percentage of time spent on each. The letter should outline of all the beneficiary's positions while employed with the foreign entity, along with job descriptions and employment dates at any affiliated entities, if applicable. It must also specifically explain how beneficiary's prior education, training, and employment qualify him/her to perform the intended services in the U.S, even if the work abroad is not the same as proposed U.S. employment.
        i. **In addition, the letter must contain the following information below, as appropriate to the position:**

1. *For managerial positions* – explain how the beneficiary manages the organization, department, subdivision, function, or component of organization; supervises and controls work of other supervisory, professional, or managerial employees; has authority to hire and fire or recommend personnel actions (i.e. promotion and leave authorization); and makes decisions on daily operations of the activity or function under his/her authority.
    1. If beneficiary is a first line supervisor, documentation that he/she supervises professionals (i.e. with bachelor degrees or equivalent)
2. *For executive positions* – explain how the beneficiary directs management of the organization, or a major component or function of the organization; establishes goals and policies of the organization, component, or function; exercises wide latitude in discretionary decision-making; and receives only general supervision or direction from higher level executives, board of directors, or stockholders, if applicable.
3. *For functional manager positions* – explain how the beneficiary manages an "essential" function of the company, and that that the function is a clearly defined activity and essential or core to the organization. Must also demonstrate that the beneficiary primarily manages as opposed to performs, the function; the beneficiary acts at a senior level within the organizational hierarchy or with respect to the function managed; and that the beneficiary exercises discretion over the function's day-to-day operations.

b. Organizational charts
  i. Chart(s) or diagram(s) demonstrating the foreign entity's organizational structure and staffing levels, clearly indicating beneficiary's position in the chart, along with name/title of direct supervisor, peers, and subordinates, explaining the relationship between each.
c. A complete list of all employees in beneficiary's immediate group, division, or department, including their name, job title, summary of duties and minimum requirements for the position, along with the respective salary and educational level for each individual;
d. Copies of any appraisals or performance reviews conducted by beneficiary for subordinate employees, if applicable; and
e. Copies of beneficiary's training, personnel records, or any other documentation showing transferee's capability to conduct business in executive or managerial capacity.

Documents from U.S. Company:

1. Information on proposed position in the U.S. - work address, annual salary and any benefits (indicate whether salary will be paid by U.S. or foreign employer), and estimated start date for position in U.S.;
2. Name, title, address and telephone number for signatory;

3. Current number of employees;
4. Articles and Certificate of Incorporation, and By-Laws or other corporate documents;
5. Stock certificates;
6. Stock Transfer Ledger;
7. Most recent Federal Income Tax Returns and/or audited financial statements, if applicable;
8. Most recent annual report filed by U.S. entity, which lists all parent companies, affiliates, subsidiaries, and branch offices, and documents percentage of ownership or most recent Securities and Exchange commission Form 10-K, if applicable;
9. Lease for place of business in the United States for at least 1 year, signed and dated by all parties;
10. Ten photographs of interior and exterior of building in the United States (place of business);
11. Evidence that the beneficiary's proposed employment in the U.S. is managerial or executive in nature:
    a. Letter from high-level manager or executive in U.S. entity describing how beneficiary will be employed in qualifying, managerial position, with detailed description of job duties and percentage of time to be spent on each. **In addition, include the relevant information below, as appropriate to the position:**
        1. *For managerial positions* – describe how beneficiary will manage the organization, department, subdivision, function, or component of organization; will supervise and control work of other supervisory, professional, or managerial employees; will have the authority to hire and fire or recommend personnel actions (i.e. promotion and leave authorization); and will make decisions on daily operations of the activity or function under his authority.
            a) If beneficiary will be first line supervisor, documentation that he/she will be supervising professionals (i.e. with bachelor degrees or equivalent)
        2. *For executive positions* – explain how the beneficiary will direct management of the organization, or a major component or function of the organization; will establish goals and policies of the organization, component, or function; will exercise wide latitude in discretionary decision-making; and will receive only general supervision or direction from higher level executives, board of directors, or stockholders, if applicable.
        3. *For functional manager positions* – explain how the beneficiary will manage an "essential" function of the company, and that that the function is a clearly defined activity and essential or core to the organization. Must also demonstrate that the beneficiary will primarily manage as opposed to perform, the function; the beneficiary will act at a senior level within the organizational hierarchy or with respect to the function managed; and that the beneficiary will exercise discretion over the function's day-to-day operations.
    b. Organizational charts
        1. Chart(s) or diagram(s) demonstrating the U.S. entity's organizational structure and staffing levels, clearly indicating beneficiary's position in the chart, along with name/title of direct supervisor, peers, and subordinates, explaining the relationship between each.
    c. A complete list of all employees in beneficiary's immediate group, division, or department, including their name, job title, summary of duties and minimum

       requirements for the position, along with the respective salary and educational level for each individual;
- d. Copies of State Quarterly Wage Report for most recent, accepted quarter;
- e. Copies of U.S. entities' payroll summary, Forms W-2, W-3, and 1099-MISC showing wages paid to all employees who will be under beneficiary's direction; and
- f. Copies of employment agreements entered into by any newly hired employees who will be managed by beneficiary, if applicable.

Documents from Individual/Foreign National:

1. Completed NIV Questionnaire from Kuck Immigration Partners LLC;
2. Photocopies of individual's passport, visa, and Form I-94 (www.; https://i94.cbp.dhs.gov);
3. Photocopies of individual's university or trade school diplomas, licenses, and certificates, with course transcripts;
4. Individual's resume, curriculum vitae, etc.;
5. Photocopy of most recently available governmental income tax withholding form (U.S. "W 2" Wage and Tax Withholding Statement, Canadian "T 4," British "P60" or Australian "Group Certificate", or similar foreign tax authority document) showing year, name of foreign employer, name of employee, salary paid, tax withheld, etc; OR pay statements for one year;
6. Photocopy of individual's Form I-797 Notice of Action evidencing current approved visa status in the United States, if applicable;
7. Employment Verification Letter - letter from individual's employer overseas indicating his/her job title and the month/year he/she commenced employment and detailed description of his/her current job duties with overseas employees – include number and title of any subordinate employees; and
8. If any immediate family members will accompany him/her to the United States – photocopies of passport pages, visa, Form I-94 card, current and prior Form I-797 Notice of Approval evidencing prior visa statuses, marriage certificate, and birth certificate of children

** ALL FOREIGN LANGUAGE DOCUMENTS MUST BE ACCOMPANIED BY CERTIFED ENGLISH TRANSLATION **

KBI Client Document Checklist for new L-1B Visa

DOCUMENT CHECKLIST FOR NEW L-1B VISA

List of Required Documents from Foreign Company

1. Articles of Incorporation, or equivalent from official source (such as city or province with which the business is registered);
2. Copies of ownership documents (stock certificates or other documents that list the owners of the business or the shares of the business);
3. Company organization chart documenting the relationship between the foreign and U.S. company;
4. Current number of employees;
5. Evidence that the foreign company has been doing business for 1 year or longer:
   a. Most recent Annual Report or audited Financial Statement/Balance Sheet
   b. Most recent business tax return
   c. Copies of payroll records (showing applicant as an employee), including payroll ledger and proof of payment of salaries to employees (must be more than 2 employees) for the past year – at least one record per quarter
   d. Local business or occupational licenses or equivalent
   e. Recent bank statements (for the past year)
   f. Copy of lease or deed to premises, valid for at least 1 year (signed and dated by all parties)
   g. Purchase orders, invoices, bills of lading, etc.(for the past year)
   h. Ten photographs (either 3x5 or 4x6) of the interior and exterior of the Company's office, factories, buildings, etc. and photos of employees working there
6. Evidence of the beneficiary's employment for a minimum of 1 year in the past 3 years in a specialized knowledge position
   a. Company statement - Letter on company letterhead from high-level manager or executive in foreign business confirming beneficiary's employment in specialized knowledge position abroad, including the specific job duties/functions and the percentage of time spent on each. The letter must specifically describe the beneficiary's advanced expertise and his or her specialized/proprietary knowledge or training. In this regard, the letter should:
      i. *Describe all of the position(s) the beneficiary has held with the company along with discussion of training, work experience, or education establishing the number of years the individual has been using or developing the claimed specialized knowledge as an employee of the petitioning organization or in the industry;*
      ii. *Identify which of the petitioning organization's products, services, tools, research, equipment, techniques, management, or processes and procedures involved in the beneficiary's job duties require specialized knowledge;*
      iii. *Explain how the beneficiary's knowledge or expertise identified was either "special" or "advanced"; how and at what point the beneficiary obtained this special or advanced knowledge;*
      iv. *State the minimum time required to obtain this knowledge, including training and actual experience accrued after the completion of training;*

     v. Explain the knowledge required to perform the duties of the foreign position and how it compares to that of similarly employed individuals within the employer
    vi. Discuss the impact, if any, the transfer of the individual would have on the petitioning organization's U.S. operations; and
   vii. Describe how the beneficiary is qualified to contribute significantly to the U.S. operation's knowledge of foreign operating conditions as a result of knowledge not generally found in the petitioning organization's U.S. operations.

  b. **Documentation of specialized knowledge, including but not limited to:**
     i. Documentation of training, work experience, or education establishing the number of years the individual has been using or developing the claimed specialized knowledge as an employee of the petitioning organization or in the industry
    ii. Contracts, statements of work, or other documentation that shows that the beneficiary possesses knowledge that is particularly beneficial to the petitioning organization's competitiveness in the marketplace
   iii. Evidence, such as correspondence or reports, establishing that the beneficiary has been employed abroad in a capacity involving assignments that have significantly enhanced the petitioning organization's productivity, competitiveness, image, or financial position
   iv. Personnel or in-house training records that establish that the beneficiary's claimed specialized knowledge normally can be gained only through prior experience or training with the petitioning organization
    v. Curricula and training manuals for internal training courses, financial documents, or other evidence that may demonstrate that the beneficiary possesses knowledge of a product or process that cannot be transferred or taught to another individual without significant economic cost or inconvenience
   vi. Evidence of patents, trademarks, licenses, or contracts awarded to the petitioning organization based on the beneficiary's work, or similar evidence that the beneficiary has knowledge of a process or a product that either is sophisticated or complex, or of a highly technical nature, although not necessarily proprietary or unique to the petitioning organization

  c. **Organizational charts for position abroad**
     i. Chart(s) or diagram(s) demonstrating the foreign entity's organizational structure and staffing levels, clearly indicating beneficiary's position in the chart, along with name/title of direct supervisor, peers, and subordinates, explaining the relationship between each.

List of Required Documents from U.S. Company

1. Information on proposed position in the U.S. - work address, annual salary and any benefits (indicate whether salary will be paid by U.S. or foreign employer), and estimated start date for position in U.S.;
2. Current number of employees;
3. Name, title, address, and telephone number for signatory;
4. Articles and Certificate of Incorporation and By-laws and other corporate documents;

5. Stock certificates or Stock transfer ledger;
6. Most recent annual report filed by U.S. entity, which lists all parent companies, affiliates, subsidiaries, and branch offices, and documents percentage of ownership or most recent Securities and Exchange commission Form 10-K, if applicable;
7. Current business registration/license as applicable (i.e., city, state, county, or federal);
8. **Financial and tax supporting documents**
    a. most recent audited Financial Statements/year to-date financials
    b. most recent corporate tax return
    c. employer's wage and tax report
    d. 941 quarterly statements for most recent tax year
9. **Evidence of current U.S. operations**
    a. Recent bank statements (for the past year)
    b. Sales Invoices, Purchase orders, bills of lading (for the past year)
    c. Copy of lease or deed to premises (signed and dated by all parties)
    d. Ten photographs (either 3x5 or 4x6) of the interior and exterior of the Company's office, factories, buildings, etc.
    e. Vendor, supplier, or customer contracts
    f. Third party license agreements
    g. Brochures/advertisements
10. Evidence that the beneficiary's proposed employment in the U.S. will be in a <u>specialized knowledge</u> position:
    a. **Company statement** - Letter from high-level manager or executive in U.S. entity describing how beneficiary will be employed in qualifying, specialized knowledge position, with detailed description of job duties <u>and</u> percentage of time to be spent on each. In particular, the letter should discuss:
        i. *The specific nature of the industry or field involved;*
        ii. *The nature of the petitioning organization's products or services- describe the products, services, tools, research, equipment, techniques, management, or processes and procedures of the petitioning organization of which the beneficiary has specialized knowledge;*
        iii. *The nature of specialized knowledge required to perform the beneficiary's proposed duties and explanation of how the knowledge or expertise identified is special and/or advanced; How does this compare to that of similarly employed individuals within the employer and the industry in general?;*
        iv. *The minimum amount of time required to obtain this knowledge, including training and actual experience accrued after the completion of training; and*
        v. *The need for beneficiary's specialized knowledge, especially if other employees have the same or similar knowledge.*
    b. **Organizational charts**
        i. Chart(s) or diagram(s) demonstrating the U.S. entity's organizational structure and staffing levels, clearly indicating beneficiary's position in the chart, along with name/title of direct supervisor, peers, and subordinates, explaining the relationship between each.
11. **Will the beneficiary be coming to the U.S. to help start a new office? If so, please provide:**
    a. Details on how company plans to staff office with U.S. workers, how L-1 assignment benefits long-term goals of U.S. business, detailed personnel structure, financial goals, etc.

    b. Evidence showing authorization and/or transfer of funds to the U.S. company from the foreign firm
        i. Money transfer documents from foreign company directly to U.S. company bank account (we suggest approximately $5,000 to $20,000);
        ii. Bank letter or statement showing money has been received; and
        iii. If the U.S. Company has been doing business for one year, we need transactional documentation showing this - invoices, bills of lading, customs receipts, etc.
    c. Business plan from a certified public accountant or company executive (we suggest using a computer program called BIZPLAN to prepare this document)

Individual/Applicant Information

1. Completed NIV Questionnaire from Kuck Immigration Partners LLC;
2. Photocopies of individual's passport, visa, and Form I-94 (https://i94.cbp.dhs.gov);
3. Photocopies of individual's university or trade school diplomas with course transcripts, licenses or certificates documenting specialized knowledge and training;
4. Individual's resume, curriculum vitae, etc.;
5. Photocopy of most recently available governmental income tax withholding form (U.S. "W 2" Wage and Tax Withholding Statement, Canadian "T 4," British "P60" or Australian "Group Certificate", or similar foreign tax authority document) showing year, name of foreign employer, name of employee, salary paid, tax withheld, etc; OR pay statements for one year;
6. Photocopy of individual's Form I-797 Notice of Action evidencing current approved visa status in the United States, if applicable;
7. Employment Verification Letter - letter from individual's employer overseas indicating his/her job title and the month/year he/she commenced employment and detailed description of his/her job duties with overseas employer; and
8. If any immediate family members will accompany him/her to the United States – photocopies of passport pages, visa, Form I-94 card, current and prior Form I-797 Notice of Approval evidencing prior visa statuses, marriage certificate, and birth certificate of children

*** ALL FOREIGN LANGUAGE DOCUMENTS MUST BE ACCOMPANIED BY CERTIFED ENGLISH TRANSLATION ***

KBI Process and Procedures Memo for EB-2 NIW

EB-2 NIW PROCESSING AND INFORMATION
THROUGH KUCK BAXTER LLC
ckuck@immigration.net

The types of evidence submitted in support of your application fall into three categories: *testimonial* (reference letters that explain your achievements and their significance in your field), *corroborating* (copies of documentation that established your achievements, such as publications or awards), and *cover letter* explaining your eligibility for the petition seeking.

I. PREPARING FOR TESTIMONIAL EVIDENCE

A. Provide a list of referees with their contact information and brief description about how you know the referees.
B. Letters of reference templates for each of your referees will be drafted by our office with the information you provide about your expertise and the reference.
C. You provide information in the form of a "personal statement", samples of which are attached. This statement is for our internal use only, and is not included in nor submitted with the petition. It is merely for our records, to provide significant details for us to draft letters.
D. Note that this petition is not a peer-review process; therefore information provided should be comprehensible to the "average person".
E. Your personal statement should be provided in electronic format (visa email), with your most up-to-date CV attached, also in electronic format.
F. Our office will draft 5 reference letter templates. Once these reference letters are drafted they will be sent to you to review for accuracy.
G. Once the reference letters are finalized, we will send them to your referees, to be reviewed, printed on letterhead, and signed. We will advise your referees to attach their full CV to establish their credentials.

IMPORTANT! Selecting Appropriate Referees
- Letter of reference convey the weight of your achievements.
- Letter from prestigious institutions that make a stronger impact on your case.
- Geographical and institutional diversity is important.
- A referee should be an objective independent source: referee does not have to know you personally; it may be better if they only know you by your reputation.

II. CORROBORATING DOCUMENTATION

A. This documentation needs to be submitted to our office as hard copies, in addition to electronic files if available.
B. This primary source documentation will corroborate the information detailed in your personal statement and in the letters.

C. Your CV is not considered evidence. If something is important enough to be on your CV, you should provide us with the primary source evidence.
D. Translations – Regulations require any document not submitted in English to be translated. Word-for-word translations of short documents are necessary.
   *Translation should be attached to un-translated documents. We will advise you regarding longer documents, such as articles and manuscripts.
E. Copies are always sufficient; we do not need originals.
F. The more corroborating documentation the better, so send everything you can and we will sort through and decide what to use.
   - Examples:
     1. Degree/diploma certificates;
     2. Patents, Trademarks and Copyrights;
     3. Awards/Honors, including the criteria for the award or honors;
     4. Grant Applications/Awards, including the criteria for the grant or award;
     5. Professional memberships/criteria for membership;
     6. Publications;
     7. Publication citations;
     8. Abstract presentations;
     9. Evidence that you have served as a reviewer and/or judge of others' work;
     10. Invitation letters and emails to professional meetings and memberships;
     11. Request for reprints;
     12. Media Coverage on you and your work (print or online);
     13. Evidence of your original scientific, scholarly, artistic, or business-related contributions of major significance to the field;
     14. Performance of a leading or critical role in distinguished organizations;
     15. Employment verification letter stating your current job title and annual salary if available;
     16. Evidence of job offers in your field;
     17. Contracts, agreements, or licenses showing potential impact of your work;
     18. Evidence you have received investment from U.S. investors;
     19. Letters from government agencies or quasi-govt entities in US demonstrating you are positioned to advance your endeavor;
     20. Evidence of non-monetary support from govt. entities with expertise in economic development, R&D, or job creation;
     21. Evidence your work will lead to U.S. job creation; and
     22. Evidence your work is being used by others.

Even if you do not have a document, please still include the information in your personal statement.

IMPORTANT! Preparing Corroborating Documentation

A. PUBLICATIONS
   1. Provide copies of all first author & last (senior) author article (entire articles)
   2. For books authored or edited, full copies are not needed. Provide copies of the book's title and the table of contents.
   3. Any documents not in English, must have a copy of the original

version with attached certified translation (just an abstract and title).

B. PRESENTATIONS
1. Provide copies of all published abstracts.
2. Provide copies of all conference proceedings, or conference brochure highlighting your presentation.
3. Provide copies of emails or letters regarding acceptance, invitation, or appreciation.
4. Any documents not in English, must have a copy of the original version with attached certified translation (just an abstract and title).

C. PUBLISHED MATERIALS ABOUT APPLICANT
Citations & reference to your work/findings; acknowledgements to you or your work; websites discussing your work; press releases about your work; discussion of your work in the media; newspaper articles about you or your work; and newsletters mentioning you and your contribution to the field.
1. Provide copies of any material notes above.
2. Highlight where you or your work is referenced/discussed.
3. Include printouts from websites that discuss you/your work.
4. Citations:
    - For each of your publications, provide a complete official list of citations to your work. These lists should be directly printed out from an official search engine (e.g. Web of Science, Scopus, SciFinder, and etc.) Provide a separate list for each publication, which refers to that publication, shows the total number of citations to that publication, and lists the title of each citing article.
    - **Highlight** where in the article it discusses your work, and where your name is listed.

D. LEADING AND CRITICAL ROLES (EMPLOYMENT HISTORY)
1. Appointment letters/emails;
2. Copies of Contracts;
3. Offer letters.

E. JUDGE OF THE WORK OF OTHERS
Manuscript/peer reviewer/grant reviewer; review articles/textbook chapters; editorials/letters to the editor; moderator/chair of presentations/panels; advisory boards/committees; or seat on editorial board.

IMPORTANT! Documentation:
- Emails/letters acknowledging role;
- Copies of editorials/chapters/reviews noting authorship;
- For textbooks, do not provide the entire book. Provide the table of contents and your chapter/article;
- Website printouts noting your role/title/position;
- Excerpt from conference brochure noting position as moderator, etc.

F. HONORS AND AWARDS
   1. Provide selection criteria/process for selection
      - What was the basis for the award?
      - What entity granted the award?
      - With whom were you in competition?
      - How many of such awards were granted?
      - Any publicity for the award?
   2. Example of Awards
      - Research funding in your name;
      - Travel grants to attend or present at conference;
      - Best presentation/poster;

   IMPORTANT! Documentation:
   - Copies of the award, copies of selection criteria;
   - Copies of the grant, listing you as an investigator;
   - Copies of patent submissions/awards;
   - Copies of publicity for the award.

G. MEMBERSHIP IN SOCIETIES THAT REQUIRE A LEVEL OF ACHIEVEVEMENT; SOCIETIES THAT REQUIRE MORE THAN PAYING A FEE.
   1. Academic honor societies;
   2. Certifying societies;
   3. Societies that require nomination and/or election consider:
      - What are the criteria for obtaining membership?
      - What is the selection process?
      - How many members does the society have?

   IMPORTANT! Documentation:
   - Proof of membership.
   - Copy of blank application used to apply for the membership
   - Documentation of membership criteria (from website).

III. PROCESS FOR PREPARING COVER LETTER

   A. Letters of cover letter will be drafted by our office according to the information you provide about your expertise.
   B. Once the cover letter is drafted, it will be sent to you to review for accuracy.

If you would like further information about specific case scenarios or situations, please call our office or email us at ckuck@immigration.net to speak to one of our experienced immigration attorneys.

DISCLAIMER: The confidential information provided in this memorandum is for information purposes only and is not intended to be legal advice. This information is not intended to create an attorney-client or other relationship between Kuck Baxter Immigration LLC and the recipient. The reader should consult with an immigration attorney before acting in reliance on any such information.

Labor Certification: List of Required Documents (LR and SM Revised)

SUPPORT DOCUMENTATION FOR LABOR CERTIFICATION APPLICATION

A. CORPORATE (Prospective U.S. Employer):

1. Completed Employer/Sponsor Labor Certification Questionnaire
2. Certificate and Articles of Incorporation
3. Employer's Federal Tax Identification Number
4. Current annual report and/or audited financial statement, or federal corporate income tax return
5. Lease or deed for business premises
6. Any available promotional pamphlets and brochures which describe the company and its various products, service, etc.
7. A complete job description for the individual's proposed position — including title, list of all job duties; title of immediate supervisor, number and title of persons supervised, and annual salary and benefits information; and
8. Full name and title of contact person at company who will coordinate paperwork and the full name, title, email, and telephone number of the company's authorized signatory for documents.

B. INDIVIDUAL (Foreign National)

1. Completed General Immigration Questionnaire and Completed Labor Certification Questionnaire
2. Photocopies of individual's passport and those of his immediate family members who will accompany him to the United States
3. Photocopies of individual's immigration documentation, including visas, I-797 approval notices, I-20, DS-2019, EAD's, and any other documentation
4. Individual's resume, curriculum vitae, etc.
5. Photocopy of individual's university or trade school diplomas and certificates, and course transcripts, if available
6. Photocopy of individual's professional licenses, professional society membership certificates or cards, etc; and
7. Any available reference letters verifying the individual's prior work history

If possible, English translations should be provided for any foreign language documents.

If you would like further information about specific case scenarios or situations, please call our office or email us at ckuck@immigration.net to speak to one of experienced immigration attorneys.

Kuck | Baxter LLC · Atlanta · www.immigration.net
365 Northridge Road, Suite 300, Atlanta, GA 30350 · T 404.816.8611 · T 866.286.6200 · F 404.816.8615

THE NEXT STEP

To schedule an appointment with Attorney Charles Kuck or any of his partners and associates, please visit our website or call us at (404) 816-8611.

INDEX

D

DACA status · 94

E

E-2 investor visa · 47
E-2 non-immigrant investment visas · 44
E-2 Non-Immigrant Investor Program · 39
E-2 non-immigrant visa program · 44
EB-2 national interest waivers · 63
EB-2 visas · 58
EB-2A visa · 62
EB-3 visa category · 65
EB-5 cases · 53
EB-5 Immigrant Investor Program · 39
EB-5 investor program · 33
EB-5 permanent conditional resident green card · 41
EB-5 petitions · 33
EB-5 visas · 41

F

fiancé visas · 82

H

H-1B visas · 34
H2B visa · 37

I

immigration to the United States · 49

L

L-1 Visa for Intra-company Transferees · 39
L-1 visas · 47
L-1A visa extension · 48
L1A visas · 44

M

MME immigrant visa · 48

O

O-1 extraordinary ability visas · 25

P

permanent residence · 42

Notes